Dad's College Advice

j.a. naumann

For my children whom I love.
And the other one too.

SmartMouth™ Original Activated Mouthwash used by permission from SmartMouth™ Oral Health Laboratories. Thanks Andy!

i

Special thanks to Melissa for taking time to proof read and edit my slop. If you find any mistakes they are because I chose to ignore her corrections, and put the slop back in.

I've always believed that
when you find yourself in a stressful situation,
you can choose to laugh,
or you can choose to cry.

I prefer to laugh.

This book is for those who also prefer to laugh,
even if it is more likely to make them cry.

A BIT OF DAD'S COLLEGE ADVICE

A vampire student at the University of Transylvania came into the vampire student union covered in fresh blood and parked himself in a corner coffin to get some sleep. Pretty soon all the other vampire students saw the blood and began excitedly asking him where he got it. He told them to knock it off and let him get some sleep, but they persisted until he finally he gave in.

"Okay, follow me," he said, and he ran out of the building with dozens of other vampire students following him. They flew past the rec center, around the football stadium, through the quad, and then into a campus green space full of trees.

Finally, he slowed down, and the other vampire students excitedly circled around him. "Now do you see that crooked elm tree over there?" he asked.

"Yes! Yes! Yes!" the other vampires all screamed in a frenzy.

"Good," said the first vampire. "Because I didn't!"

Moral of the story: Be watchful walking around campus at night.

MORE DAD'S COLLEGE ADVICE

Joe, a college student, gets a cash gift from his mother. He decides to go out and treat himself to some ice cream. Half an hour later, he returns.

"So Joe, what did you do?" asks his mother.

Joe replies "I went out to the ice cream parlor and bought myself an ice cream."

"Oh, that's nice," says his mother. "What flavor did you get?"

Joe says, "Strawberry."

Joe's mother explodes, "Strawberry?!? Why, you little liar! Just wait until your father gets home!"

A few hours later, Joe's father comes home. The mother says, "You would not believe what Joe told me. He needs to be punished."

Joe's father says, "OK, calm down. Joe, what happened?"

Joe says "Mom gave me my allowance, so I went out to the ice cream parlor and bought myself an ice cream. Then I came home, and Mom asked me what flavor of ice cream I got. I told her, and she got really mad!"

Dad says, "Really? That's pretty unreasonable. Joe, you didn't do anything wrong. You are not in trouble. By the way, what flavor did you get?"

"Strawberry," Joe replies.

His dad exploded at him, "You little hooligan! How dare you lie to me? I'm so mad, I'm calling the cops!"

A few minutes later, the cops arrive. "OK, son, tell us your side of the story."

Joe says, "Mom gave me my allowance, so I went out to the ice cream parlor and bought myself an ice cream. Then I came home, and Mom asked me what flavor of ice cream I got. I told her, and she got really mad! So when Dad got home, I told him what happened, and he got so mad that he called you! Are you going to arrest me?"

The cops glared at Joe's parents. "Sir, 911 is for serious emergencies only. We don't have time to investigate petty complaints like these. Please do not waste out time like this. Another call like this and we'll have to write you a ticket."

"So I'm not in trouble?" asks Joe.

"No, son, you're not in trouble. By the way, what flavor ice cream did you get?"

"Strawberry."

"On the ground, NOW! Hands behind your head! Move it, scumbag!" The cops proceed to taser the heck out of Joe.

Months later, Joe is in court. The judge asks "What is this case about?" The defense attorney begins, "Your honor, my client is completely innocent. He got his allowance from his mother, proceeded to the ice cream parlor, had ice cream, and returned home. Any reasonable person would conclude that this is a perfectly reasonable course of action for any young man. And yet, he was arrested, beaten, and tasered by the arresting officers. We ask that all charges be dropped. Furthermore, we ask that charges be brought against the arresting officers."

The judge asks the prosecution for his opening statement. "Your honor, the prosecution has no case. We request that the case be dismissed."

The judge addresses Joe. "Son, the state apologizes for any inconvenience that this misunderstanding has caused. You are free to go."

Dad's College Advice

Joe smiles, gets up, and turns to leave the courthouse. The judge says, "You're a good boy. I like ice cream too. By the way, what flavor did you get."

Joe mumbles, "Strawberry."

"Boy, I could have you hanged for that! But rope is too good for you. I never, ever, want to see you again. You are to leave town, and never return. You disgust me. If you ever step foot in this town again, I will personally see to it that you get the death penalty."

Completely dejected, Joe leaves the courthouse. As he is crossing the street, he gets run over by a reckless driver and is killed.

Moral of the story: Look both ways before crossing the street.

MORE DAD'S COLLEGE ADVICE

A linguistics professor was lecturing to his class one day.

"In English," he said, "a double negative forms a positive. In some languages, though, such as Russian, a double negative is still a negative. However," he pointed out, "there is no language wherein a double positive can form a negative."

A contrarian student from the back of the room piped up and said, "Yeah, right."

Moral of the story: Proofread and check your grammar when writing essays. Always remember that double negatives are a no-no.

MORE DAD'S COLLEGE ADVICE

A student takes his Rottweiler to the vet.

"Can you have a look at him," he says, "I think he's cross-eyed."

So the vet picks up the dog and examines him. "I'm going to have to put him down," says the vet.

"Why, just because he's cross eyed?"

"No," says the vet, "because he's heavy!"

Moral of the story: If you have a teacher with crossed eyes, be nice and behave extra good in class because teachers like that sometimes have trouble controlling their pupils.

MORE DAD'S COLLEGE ADVICE

Mary Poppins moved to California and started a business telling college students their fortunes. She didn't read palms or tea leaves, instead she smelled the student's breath.

The sign outside her office read: "Super California Mystic, Expert Halitosis."

Moral of the story: Make sure you use your SmartMouth™ Original Activated Mouthwash every day.

MORE DAD'S COLLEGE ADVICE

A student goes to a night club; the bouncer stops him. "No tie, no entry."

He walks back to his car to find a tie. All he finds are jumper cables, so he puts them around his neck like a tie.

He goes back and says, "How's this?"

The bouncer says, "I'll let you in, but don't start anything."

Moral of the story: Make sure to dress appropriately for the occasion.

MORE DAD'S COLLEGE ADVICE

Philosophy class teaches that student who runs behind car will get exhausted, but student who runs in front of car will get tired.

Moral of the story: Sometimes you have to choose the lesser of two bad options, or maybe just don't try to run with cars.

MORE DAD'S COLLEGE ADVICE

There was a college student who tried to warn them about the Titanic.

He screamed and shouted about the iceberg and how the ship was going to sink, but all they did was throw him out of the theater.

Moral of the story: Know what you're talking about before going off on a rant. And never go to see a chick flick disguised as a disaster movie.

MORE DAD'S COLLEGE ADVICE

A professor had left his students in the lab as they started on a new project, when suddenly he saw bright flashes of light and heard loud booming noises coming from the lab. In a panic he ran back into the lab, terrified of the disastrous scene that he was sure awaited him.

He burst into the lab flabbergasted to see everything in proper order, his students gathered around a lab table having a lively discussion. The perplexed professor stared dumbfounded at the students and asked them about the brilliant flashes of light and deafening booms that had come from the room.

"Oh, that," replied one of the students nonchalantly, "we were just in here brainstorming."

Moral of the story: Let your teacher know if you're stuck brainstorming. They might have a good suggestion to help get you started.

MORE DAD'S COLLEGE ADVICE

When NASA was preparing for the Apollo project, some of the training of the astronauts took place on a Navajo reservation. One day, a Navajo elder and his college student son came across the space crew.

The old man, who spoke only Navajo, asked a question that his son translated. "What are these guys in the big suits doing?"

After member of the crew said they were practicing for their trip to the moon, the old man got all excited and asked if he could send a message to the moon with the astronauts. Recognizing a promotional opportunity, the NASA folks found a tape recorder.

After the old man recorded his message, they asked his son to translate it. He refused. The NASA PR people brought the tape to the reservation, where the rest of the tribe listened and laughed, but refused to translate the elder's message.

Finally, the NASA crew called in an official government translator. His translation of the old man's message was: "Watch out for these guys; they have come to steal your land."

Moral of the story: If someone ever tells you that the sky is the limit, you can prove them wrong by becoming an astronaut.

MORE DAD'S COLLEGE ADVICE

And the Lord said unto John, "Come forth and you will receive eternal life." John came fifth and won a toaster.

Moral of the story: If you don't follow the Lord's instructions, you might end up a little toasty.

MORE DAD'S COLLEGE ADVICE

A student went to the bank, where an elderly lady asked him to help check her balance. So he pushed her over.

Moral of the story: Sometimes it's good to ask for clarification so you know what the teacher is really asking for.

MORE DAD'S COLLEGE ADVICE

A student got permission to keep a comfort animal with her on campus, so she brought her dog from home. Every morning she would take the dog out to the campus greenways. Unfortunately the dog used to chase people on a bike a lot. It got so bad, she finally had to take his bike away.

Moral of the story: Be respectful of others when playing with your toys, or someone will likely take them away from you.

MORE DAD'S COLLEGE ADVICE

A student was telling his roommate that he once had a cow with no legs. His incredulous roommate asked him, "Now where on earth do you find a cow with no legs?!?"

The student replied, "Right where you left it."

Moral of the story: If you put your stuff away properly, you'll have no trouble finding it when you want it..

MORE DAD'S COLLEGE ADVICE

A student tried explaining to his professor that he didn't have enough time to complete his homework because he had eaten a clock, and it was very time consuming.

Moral of the story: Don't wait until the last minute to get things done.

MORE DAD'S COLLEGE ADVICE

A college student was having a conversation with a classmate who happened to be blind. The blind classmate was telling her about how blind people liked to do many of the same things that are enjoyed by people blessed with normal sight.

She asked her classmate if blind people ever did things like skydiving.

"Oh, no. All blind people hate skydiving," her classmate answered.

"Well, why do all blind people hate skydiving?" she asked.

He answered, "Because it scares the hell out of the dogs!"

Moral of the story: Don't assume someone's reason for disliking something. It may be different than you think.

MORE DAD'S COLLEGE ADVICE

After class one day, a blind student walks into a bar. And a table. And a chair.

If only he hadn't scared his dog so bad with that skydiving stunt . . .

Moral of the story: Be nice to everyone. You never know when you might need their assistance.

MORE DAD'S COLLEGE ADVICE

A student went to see his school baseball team play.

He was watching from the bleachers and couldn't figure out why the baseball kept getting larger. Then it hit him.

Moral of the story: If you don't pay attention to your surroundings you might get hit with an unpleasant surprise.

MORE DAD'S COLLEGE ADVICE

A student walks into a library and asks if they have any books about paranoia.

The librarian says, "They're right behind you!"

Moral of the story: Keep calm and ask follow up questions; people might not be saying what you think you're hearing.

MORE DAD'S COLLEGE ADVICE

A student noticed that his roommate had been in a funk the last few days. So he asked, "Why have you been acting so weird lately?"

His roommate answered, "The other day, my girlfriend asked me to pass her lipstick, but I accidentally passed her a glue stick. She still isn't talking to me."

Moral of the story: Always make sure to read labels and instructions.

MORE DAD'S COLLEGE ADVICE

At the start of classes one day the professor told her class, "I just wrote a book on reverse psychology. Do *not* read it!"

Moral of the story: If your teacher wrote a book on the subject of the class, it's a good idea to make sure you read it.

MORE DAD'S COLLEGE ADVICE

A man is waiting for his wife to give birth. The doctor comes in and informs the dad that his son was born without a torso, arms or legs. The boy is just a head!

But the dad loves his son and raises him as well as he can, with love and compassion, and even sends the boy off to college.

While away at school the boy reaches his 21st birthday. Now the boy is old enough for his first drink.

His roommate takes him out to the local college bar, and orders up the biggest, strongest drink for his buddy.

With all the bar patrons looking on curiously, and the bartender shaking his head in disbelief, the boy takes his first sip of alcohol, and suddenly, Swoooop! - A torso pops out!

The bar is dead silent; then everyone bursts into a whoop of joy. The roommate, shocked, begs his buddy to drink again. The patrons chant, "Take another drink!"

But the bartender still shakes his head in dismay.

He takes another drink, and Swoooop! - Two arms pop out.

The bar goes wild. The roommate, hooting and hollering, begs his buddy to drink again. The patrons chant, "Take another drink!"

The bartender tries to ignore the whole affair.

By now the boy is getting tipsy, and with his new hands he reaches down, grabs his drink and guzzles the last of it, then Swoooop! - Two legs pop out.

The bar is now in euphoric chaos. The roommate falls to his knees flabbergasted.

Dad's College Advice

The boy stands up on his new legs, and starts walking, but cannot control what direction he goes, and stumbles to the left.... then to the right.... right through the front door, and into the street, where a truck runs over him and kills him instantly.

The bar falls silent. The roommate moans in grief. The bartender just shakes his head, sighs, and says, "That boy should have quit while he was a head."

Moral of the story: Make good choices; don't give in to peer pressure.

MORE DAD'S COLLEGE ADVICE

The latest celebrity on the university television station was a Russian student, going by the name of Rudolph, who had taken the weather forecasting world by storm. He seemed to have an incredible and uncanny knack of not just getting the forecast correct, but being amazingly accurate, sometimes even being able to tell where the rain would fall, down to the nearest mile or so.

His fame was enhanced by his personality - being Russian, he had some unique turns of phrase. He was also a fanatical communist.

One day, on a family weekend, a student fan was watching with her parents. She turned to her mother, and asked, "How does he manage to get the weather forecast so good?"

Her mother thought for a bit and said, "I'm not sure, but one thing's for certain - Rudolph the Red knows rain, dear."

Moral of the story: Paying attention to good weather forecasts can save you from dressing inappropriately for weather conditions.

MORE DAD'S COLLEGE ADVICE

A college student loved telling his classmates about his pet bird. It was an exotic bird species with a very distinctively shaped beak.

One day, however, the student received the sad news from home that the bird had passed away. His parents decided to memorialize the bird by keeping its beak in an ornately carved wooden box.

The student decided that the best way for him to carry on was to get another bird just like the one that had died. He didn't know what kind of bird it was, but knew it had a uniquely shaped beak, so he took the box with him to an exotic pet store.

He walked into the store and told the owner, "I want a bird that fits this beak."

"Okay," the owner replied, "I've got one that will fill the bill."

Moral of the story: Providing an example is a good way to clarify to others what you're talking about.

MORE DAD'S COLLEGE ADVICE

A college student had spent his summer working for a geology professor on excavation digs, looking for rare stone formations.

When back at school, he excitedly told his roommate, "I found a rock which measured 1760 yards in length!"

"Wow!" his roommate replied. "That must be some kind of milestone."

Moral of the story: If you give a pun teller an inch, he'll take a mile. And then you have to just "suck it up" and deal with it.

MORE DAD'S COLLEGE ADVICE

Recently, the University of Minnesota Orchestra was performing Beethoven's *Ninth Symphony* under the baton of Professor Milton Katims.

Now at this point, you must understand two things:

Firstly, there is a quite long segment in this symphony where the bass violins don't have a thing to do; not a single note for page after page.

Secondly, there is a night club right across the street from the University of Minnesota's Orchestra Hall, that was a favorite watering hole of the student musicians.

It had been decided that during this particular performance, once the bass players had played their parts in the opening of the Ninth, they were to quietly lay down their instruments and leave the stage, rather than sit on their stools looking and feeling dumb for twenty minutes.

Well, once they got backstage, someone suggested that they trot across the street and drink a few brews.

After they had downed the first couple rounds, someone said, "Shouldn't we be getting back? It'd be awfully embarrassing if we were late."

Another musician, presumably the one who suggested this excursion in the first place, replied, "Oh, I anticipated we could use a little more time, so I tied a string around the last pages of the conductor's score. When he gets down to there, Professor Katims is going to have to slow the tempo way down while he waves the baton with one hand and fumbles with the string with the other."

So they had another round, and finally returned to the Opera house, a little tipsy by now.

29

However, as they came back on stage, one look at their conductor's face told them they were in serious trouble. Professor Katims was furious! And why not?

After all ... it was the bottom of the Ninth, the basses were loaded, and the score was tied.

Moral of the story: If you don't want to upset the boss, wait to play until after the work is done.

MORE DAD'S COLLEGE ADVICE

A student, whose roommate was travelling abroad for a year, went into a pet store one day.

"I'm really lonely," she says to the clerk. "I need a pet to keep me company."

"Well," replies the clerk, "how about this nice parrot? He'll talk to you."

"Hey, that's great," says the student. She buys the parrot and takes him home.

The next day the student comes back to the pet store and says to the clerk, "You know that parrot isn't talking to me yet."

"Hmmm, let's see," says the clerk. "I know! You buy this little ladder for his cage. He'll climb the ladder, and then he'll talk."

So off the student goes with a newly purchased ladder.

But the next day she comes back to the pet store again. "Hey, that parrot still hasn't said a word," she says to the pet store clerk.

The clerk thinks for a minute. "How about this little mirror?" he says. "You hang it at the top of the ladder. The parrot will climb the ladder, look in the mirror, and then he'll talk to you."

"Okay," the student says, buys the little mirror and goes home.

But the next day that same student is back in the shop. "Well, I'm getting a bit discouraged," she says. "That parrot still won't talk to me."

The clerk scratches his head. "Let me think. Aha! Try this bell. You hang it over the mirror. The parrot will climb the ladder, look in the mirror, ring the bell, and then he will surely talk to you!"

Dad's College Advice

"All right, I'll give it a try," says the student. And she buys the bell and takes it home.

The next day the same student comes back to the pet store, and she is very distressed.

Seeing her disposition the clerk asks, "What's wrong?"

"My parrot . . . . well, he died," she answers quietly.

"Oh my gosh! I am so sorry!" exclaims the clerk. "But I have to ask you, did the parrot ever say anything to you?"

"Oh, yes. He said one thing. Right before he died," she replies.

"Well," asks the clerk, "what did he say?"

The student replies, "He said, 'Doesn't that pet store carry any bird food?'"

Moral of the story: Don't wait until you are in dire straits before asking for what you need.

MORE DAD'S COLLEGE ADVICE

One day at the end of class, Johnny's professor asked the class to go home and think of a story to be concluded with a moral of that story. The following day the professor asked for the first volunteer to tell their story.

Suzy raised her hand. "My dad owns a farm and every Sunday we load the chicken eggs on the truck and drive into town to sell them at the market. Well, one Sunday we hit a big bump and all the eggs flew out of the basket and onto the road."

When the professor asked for the moral of the story, Suzy replied, "Don't keep all your eggs in one basket."

Lucy went next. "My dad owns a farm too. Every weekend we take the chicken eggs and put them in the incubator. Last weekend only eight of the 12 eggs hatched."

Again, the professor asked for the moral of the story. Lucy replied, "Don't count your chickens before they hatch."

Next up was little Johnny. "My uncle Ted fought in the Afghanistan war, and his helicopter was shot down over enemy territory. He jumped out before it crashed but could only take a case of beer, a machine gun and a machete. On the way down, he drank the case of beer. Then he landed right in the middle of 100 Taliban soldiers. He shot 70 with his machine gun, but then he ran out of bullets! So he pulled out his machete and killed 20 more. Then the blade on his machete broke, so he killed the last ten with his bare hands."

The professor looked a little shocked. After clearing her throat, she asked what possible moral there could be to this story.

"Well," Johnny replied, "Don't mess with Uncle Ted when he's been drinking."

Moral of the story: Be watchful if someone around you has partaken liberally of alcohol; they don't always behave like normal.

MORE DAD'S COLLEGE ADVICE

A blonde student notices that her classmate has a thermos, so she asks him what it's for.

He responds, "It keeps hot things hot and cold things cold."

The blonde is impressed, and immediately goes out and buys one for herself.

The next day, she comes to class and proudly displays it.

Her classmate asks, "What do you have in it?"

She replies, "Soup and ice cream."

Moral of the story: Don't try to do two opposite things at the same time, or you'll end up with a sloppy mess.

MORE DAD'S COLLEGE ADVICE

A college student was assigned a Swiss roommate, and asked him, "What's the best thing about living in Switzerland?"

The Swiss student thought a moment, then answered, "Well, the flag is a big plus."

Moral of the story: Take advantage of opportunities to learn what others can teach you about their home.

MORE DAD'S COLLEGE ADVICE

A chess competition was being held in the student center of a university and various contestants were in the open-air lobby discussing their victories of the day.

After about an hour of this, the manager of the student center came into the lobby and asked them all to leave.

"But why?" they protested.

"Because," the manager explained, "I can't stand chess nuts boasting in an open foyer."

Moral of the story: Enjoy your victories, but don't be gloat about them.

MORE DAD'S COLLEGE ADVICE

A new professor tried to make use of her psychology background.

The first day of class, she started by saying, "Everyone who thinks they're stupid, stand up!"

After a few seconds, Little Johnny stands up.

The teacher asks, "Do you think you're stupid, Johnny?"

"No, ma'am. But I hate to see you standing there all by yourself."

Moral of the story: Sometimes the best thing is to just keep someone company.

MORE DAD'S COLLEGE ADVICE

A student who struggled with English was grateful for some assistance her roommate had given her.

She said to her roommate, "Thanks for explaining the word 'many' to me, it means a lot."

Moral of the story: Be generous with giving assistance to others, and make sure to show appreciation for assistance received.

MORE DAD'S COLLEGE ADVICE

A zoology student excitedly told his roommate, "I just watched a program about beavers. It was the best dam program I've ever seen."

Moral of the story: Always consider the context of what was said before judging its meaning.

MORE DAD'S COLLEGE ADVICE

Tired of constant blonde jokes, a blonde student dyes her hair brown. She goes for a drive in the country and sees a shepherd herding his sheep across the road.

"Hey, shepherd, if I guess how many sheep are here, can I keep one?" she asks.

The shepherd agrees. She blurts out, "352!"

The shepherd is stunned but keeps his word and allows her to pick a sheep.

"I'll take this one," she says proudly. "It's the cutest!"

"Hey lady," says the shepherd. "If I guess your real hair color, can I have my dog back?"

Moral of the story: Just be yourself because eventually others will see through any false front.

MORE DAD'S COLLEGE ADVICE

Satan appeared before a small college town congregation. Everyone started screaming and running for the front church door, trampling each other in a frantic effort to get away.

Soon everyone was gone except for an elderly gentleman professor who sat calmly.

Satan walked up to him and said, "Don't you know who I am?"

The professor replied, "Yep, sure do."

Satan asked, "Aren't you going to run?"

"Nope, sure ain't," said the professor.

Satan asked, "Why aren't you afraid of me?"

The professor replied, "Been married to your sister for over 48 years."

Moral of the story: If you want to, you can keep Satan away for 48 years by marrying his sister. But I wouldn't recommend it.

MORE DAD'S COLLEGE ADVICE

Three nuns went to a college football game, and three rambunctious students got stuck sitting behind them.

The students couldn't see very well because of the nun's little nun hats, so they came up with a plan to annoy the nuns enough to make them leave.

"I think I'll move to California, there's only 50 Catholics there," said the first student.

"I think I'll move to Washington, there's only 25 Catholics there."

"I think I'll move to Idaho, there's only 10 Catholics there."

Then one of the nuns turned around and said, "Why don't you just go to Hell, there are NO Catholics there."

Moral of the story: Don't mess with nuns.

MORE DAD'S COLLEGE ADVICE

Two college students were trying to console their roommate Susie whose dog, Skipper, had recently died.

"You know," one roommate said, "it's not so bad. Skipper's probably up in Heaven right now, having a grand old time with God."

Susie stopped crying for a moment and asked, "What would God want with a dead dog?"

Moral of the story: Be patient when consoling sad friends; sometimes their grief muddles their thinking.

MORE DAD'S COLLEGE ADVICE

College student Joe asked God, "How much is a penny worth in heaven?"

God replied, "One million dollars."

Joe asked, "How long is a minute in heaven?"

God said, "One million years."

So Joe asked God for a penny.

God said, "Sure, in a minute."

Moral of the story: Don't be greedy with God; be content that He will give you all you need, in the time that you need it.

MORE DAD'S COLLEGE ADVICE

A drunk student is walking down the street. He sees this nun, runs up and knocks her over.

He looks down at her and says, "You don't feel so tough now, do you, Batman!?"

Moral of the story: Excessive alcohol intake impairs one's judgement.

MORE DAD'S COLLEGE ADVICE

A college student told her roommate that she had just burned 2,000 calories.

"And that'll be the last time I leave brownies in the oven while I go to the gym."

Moral of the story: Make sure to turn things off before going out.

MORE DAD'S COLLEGE ADVICE

A nun walked into a bar with her clothes on inside out.

The bartender asked her about it and she replied, "Oh, it's just a bad habit."

Moral of the story: Work on building good habits.

MORE DAD'S COLLEGE ADVICE

A student asked his Irish roommate, "Why do people wear shamrocks on St. Patrick's Day?"

His roommate answered, "Because regular rocks are too heavy."

Moral of the story: Don't wear rocks, wear shamrocks.

MORE DAD'S COLLEGE ADVICE

One night, as he finished his last bit of homework, a knock came on Joe's dorm room door. He answered the door and found a six-foot cockroach standing there. The bug grabbed him by the collar and threw him across the room, then left.

The next night, came another knock on the door, and Joe found the same six-foot cockroach standing there. The big bug punched him in the stomach, then left.

The same happened the next night. This time, he was kneed in the groin, and hit behind the ear as he doubled over in pain. Then the big bug left.

The following day, Joe went to see the doctor at campus health. He explained the events of the preceding nights. "What can I do?" he pleaded.

"Not much," the doctor replied. "There's just a nasty bug going around."

Moral of the story: Cold and flu season is around the corner; plan on getting a flu shot; practice good hygiene by washing your hands often and keeping them away from your face.

MORE DAD'S COLLEGE ADVICE

Two college seniors had a week of exams coming up. They decided to party instead.

Their biggest exam was on Wednesday and they showed up telling the professor that their car had broken down the night before due to a very flat tire and that they needed a bit more time to study. The professor told them that they could have another day to study.

That evening, both of the boys crammed all night until they were sure that they knew just about everything. Arriving to class the next morning, the boys were told to go to separate classrooms to take the exam. The two of them looked at each other, shrugged and went to two different parts of the building.

As each sat down, they read the exam directions: "For 5 points, explain the contents of an atom. For 95 points, tell me WHICH tire had the flat!"

Moral of the story: Study when it's time to study; and don't try to fool your professors.

MORE DAD'S COLLEGE ADVICE

Two criminal forensics students went on a camping trip. After a good meal and a bottle of wine, they lay down for the night and went to sleep. Some hours later, the first student, Holmes, awoke and nudged his faithful friend Watson.

"Watson, look up and tell me what you see."

Watson replied, "I see millions and millions of stars."

"What does that tell you?" Holmes asked.

Watson pondered for a minute. "Astronomically, it tells me that there are millions of galaxies and potentially billions of planets. Astrologically, I observe that Saturn is in Leo. Horologically, I deduce that the time is approximately a quarter past three. Theologically, I can see that God is all powerful and that we are small and insignificant. Meteorologically, I suspect that we will have a beautiful day tomorrow. Why, what does it tell you?"

Holmes was silent for a minute, then spoke, "Watson, someone has stolen our tent."

Moral of the story: Don't make things more complicated than they need to be.

MORE DAD'S COLLEGE ADVICE

A student told her roommate one day, "When you look really closely, all mirrors look like eyeballs."

Moral of the story: Different points of reference can lead to different perspectives and different opinions of the same subject.

MORE DAD'S COLLEGE ADVICE

Jesus and Satan were having an ongoing argument about who was better on his computer. They had been going at it for days, and God was tired of hearing all of the bickering. Finally God said, "Cool it. I am going to set up a test that will run two hours and I will judge who does the better job."

So Satan and Jesus sat down at the keyboards and typed away. They moused. They did spreadsheets. They wrote reports. They sent faxes. They sent e-mails. They sent out e-mails with attachments. They downloaded. They did some genealogy reports. They made cards. They did every known job that you could do on a computer.

But ten minutes before their time was up, lightning suddenly flashed across the sky, thunder rolled, the rain poured and, of course, the electricity went off. Satan stared at his blank screen and screamed every curse word known in the underworld. Jesus just sighed.

The electricity finally flickered back on and each of them restarted their computers. Satan started searching frantically, screaming "It's gone! It's all gone! I lost everything when the power went out!" Meanwhile, Jesus quietly started printing out all of his files from the past two hours. Satan observed this and became irate. "Wait! He cheated, how did he do it?"

God just looked at him and shrugged saying, "Jesus saves."

Moral of the story: When working on the computer, save your work often.

MORE DAD'S COLLEGE ADVICE

Recently a routine police patrol was parked outside a bar frequented by college students. Late in the evening the officer noticed a student leaving the bar so intoxicated that he could barely walk. The young man stumbled around the parking lot for a few minutes, with the officer quietly observing.

After what seemed an eternity and trying his keys on five vehicles, the young man managed to find his car, which he fell into. He was there for a few minutes as most of the other patrons left the bar and drove off. Finally, he started the car, switched the wipers on and off (it wasn't raining or snowing), flicked the turn indicators on and off, tooted the horn, and then switched on the lights. He moved the vehicle forward a few inches, reversed a little, and then remained stationary for a few more minutes as more patrons pulled away in their vehicles.

At last he pulled out of the parking lot and started to drive slowly down the road. The police officer, having patiently waited all this time, now started up the patrol car, put on the flashing lights, and promptly pulled the young man over and carried out a breathalyzer test. To his amazement, the breathalyzer indicated no evidence of the young man having consumed alcohol at all!

Dumbfounded, the officer said, "I'll have to ask you to accompany me to the police station. This breathalyzer equipment must be broken."

"I doubt it," said the young man. "Tonight I'm the designated decoy."

Moral of the story: Don't drink and drive, and don't ride with a drunk driver.

MORE DAD'S COLLEGE ADVICE

Just as a surgeon was finishing up an operation and was about to close, the patient awakes, sits up, and demands to know what is going on.

"I'm about to close," the surgeon says.

The patient grabs the surgeon's hand and says, "I'm not going to let you do that! I'll close my own incision!"

The affronted doctor hands him the thread and says, "Fine, suture self."

Moral of the story: Don't be stubborn; let the professionals do what they have been trained to do.

MORE DAD'S COLLEGE ADVICE

A preacher concludes his service by saying, "Next Sunday I am going to preach on the subject of liars. And in preparation for my discourse, I would like you all to read the 17th chapter of Mark."

The following Sunday, the preacher says, "Now, all of you who have done as I requested and read the 17th chapter of Mark, please raise your hands."

Nearly every hand in the congregation goes up. The preacher continues, "You are the people I want to talk to. There is no 17th chapter of Mark."

Moral of the story: Be honest and don't tell lies; it makes it much easier to remember what you told someone.

MORE DAD'S COLLEGE ADVICE

All the monks in a certain monastery sing the simple word, "Morning" from their windows each sunrise. Early one day after several "Morning!" greetings have been sung melodiously into the dawn air, a single greeting of "Evening!" rings out of one window.

In the courtyard below, Brother Timothy looks around startled, and says, "Did you hear that, Brother Edward?"

"Hear what, Brother Timothy?" replied Brother Edward.

Brother Timothy sang in reply, "Someone chanted evening..."

Moral of the story: Don't worry about what others think; sing your own song.

MORE DAD'S COLLEGE ADVICE

Two students went to Africa for fall break and got lost in the Sahara. They had been lost in the desert for weeks, and they were at death's door. As they stumbled on, hoping for salvation in the form of an oasis or something similar, they suddenly spied, through the heat haze, a small tree off in the distance.

As they got closer, they could see that the tree was draped with rasher upon rasher of bacon. There was smoked bacon, crispy bacon, life-giving juicy nearly-raw bacon, all sorts of bacon. And the smell... oh, the glorious smell!

"Look Pepe," said the first student, "It's a bacon tree!"

"You're right!" said Pepe, "We're saved!"

Pepe didn't wait another second. He ran up to the tree salivating at the prospect of food. But just as he got to within five feet of the tree, there was the sound of machine gun fire, and he was shot down in a hail of bullets. His friend quickly dropped down on the sand, and called across to the dying Pepe.

"Pepe!! Pepe!! What on earth happened?"

And with his dying breath Pepe called back, "Run away, run!! It's not a bacon tree after all . . . . . . it's a ham bush!"

Moral of the story: Don't rush in when something looks too good to be true.

MORE DAD'S COLLEGE ADVICE

Jesus was standing on a hill preaching to his people.

"The one who hath not sinned, cast the first stone."

Just then a stone came flying from the back of the crowd and hit him hard on the head.

Jesus exclaimed, "Ouch, Mom! I hate when you do that!"

Moral of the story: Don't ever mess with your mom.

MORE DAD'S COLLEGE ADVICE

A college student rushes into a veterinarian practice, carrying the limp and lifeless body of his beloved pet gopher. The vet rushes him back to an examination room and has the student put the gopher down on the examination table. The vet examines the still, limp body and after a few moments, tells the student that his pet, regrettably is dead.

The student, clearly upset and not willing to accept the obvious, demands a second opinion. So the vet goes into the back room and comes out with a Black Labrador. The dog sniffs the body, walks from head to tail, and finally looks at the vet and barks.

The vet looks at the student and says, "I'm sorry, but the Lab thinks he's dead too."

The student is still unwilling to accept that his beloved pet is dead. So the vet brings in a Siamese cat and puts the cat down next to the gopher's body. The Siamese sniffs the body, walks from head to tail, poking and sniffing the gopher's body and finally looks at the vet and meows.

The vet looks at the student and says, "I'm sorry, but the Siamese thinks he's dead, too."

The student, finally resigned to the diagnosis, thanks the vet and asks how much he owes.

The vet answers, "$650.00."

"What!?! $650.00 just to tell me that he's dead?!" exclaims the student.

"Well," the vet replies, "the charge for my original diagnosis is $50.00. The additional $600.00 is for the lab test and cat scan."

Moral of the story: Having cats and dogs sniffing around can be very expensive.

MORE DAD'S COLLEGE ADVICE

A student tourist in Vienna is going through a graveyard and all of a sudden he hears some music. No one is around, so he starts searching for the source. He finally locates the origin and finds it is coming from a grave with a headstone that reads: Ludwig van Beethoven, 1770-1827. Then he realizes that the music is the Ninth Symphony and it is being played backward!

Puzzled, he leaves the graveyard and persuades a friend to return with him. By the time they arrive back at the grave, the music has changed. This time it is the Seventh Symphony, but like the previous piece, it is being played backward.

Curious, the students agree to consult a music scholar. When they return with the expert, the Fifth Symphony is playing, again backward. The expert notices that the symphonies are being played in the reverse order in which they were composed, the 9th, then the 7th, then the 5th.

By the next day the word has spread and a throng has gathered around the grave. They are all listening to the Second Symphony being played backward. Just then the graveyard's caretaker ambles up to the group. Someone in the crowd asks him if he has an explanation for the music.

"Oh, it's nothing to worry about," says the caretaker. "He's just decomposing."

Moral of the story: Old composers never really die; for better or worse, their music just fades away.

MORE DAD'S COLLEGE ADVICE

It's a little known fact that Quasimodo (you know - the Hunchback of Notre Dame) had an identical twin brother. The twin had left the city many years ago, to live in the countryside, where he made a good living as a bell-ringer for a small rural church.

One day, Quasimodo decides that he wants to go on a holiday - he hasn't left the city in years - so he gives his brother a ring and asks if he'd like to come over to look after the bells at Notre Dame for a week. The brother decides that this is a great idea. Nice change of scenery, and all that, so he packs a couple of bags, and heads off to Paris.

When he arrives, the first thing he notices is the size of everything. He's used to the little church bells, and the size of Notre Dame Cathedral and its bells are a little awe-inspiring. Quasimodo leads him up to the belfry.

"The bell-cords rotted through years ago," he says, "so I have to ring the bells from up here."

"How do you do that?" asks his brother (not really sure he wants to know the answer).

"Well," says Quasimodo, "I run at the bells, and hit them with my head like this...," then he takes a run at the nearest bell, and bashes it with his forehead, and it makes a beautiful (and loud) ring.

After a few demonstrations, the brother decides to have a go.

He runs up towards a bell, smacks his head against it, and it makes a lovely ring, but unfortunately, it also gives him a concussion, and he staggers around the belfry for a moment before falling out the steeple window, and down, down, down to the pavement below.

Quasimodo is understandably upset, and as he peers over the edge, he can see a crowd of people gathering around the scene.

Dad's College Advice

"Who is it?" says one.

"I'm not sure," says another, "but his face sure rings a bell."

"Yes - he's a dead ringer for Quasimodo," says a third.

"It's his brother," says another, "had a hunch he was back."

Moral of the story: Use your head for thinking, not for hammering things.

MORE DAD'S COLLEGE ADVICE

A hungry lion was roaming through the jungle looking for something to eat. He came across two men. One was sitting under a tree and reading a book; the other was typing away on his typewriter.

The lion ignored the man typing, and quickly pounced on the man reading the book and devoured him. Even the king of the jungle knows that readers digest and writers cramp.

Moral of the story: Eat right to feel right.

MORE DAD'S COLLEGE ADVICE

A highway patrolman pulled alongside a speeding car on the freeway. Glancing at the car, he was astounded to see that the blonde student behind the wheel was knitting!

Realizing that she was oblivious to his flashing lights and siren, the trooper cranked down his window, turned on his bullhorn and yelled, "Pull over!"

"NO," she yelled back over the sound of the siren, "It's a scarf!"

Moral of the story: Don't knit and drive, and don't get in a car with a driver who has been knitting.

MORE DAD'S COLLEGE ADVICE

A long time ago, there was a beehive in the middle of a forest. Every day, as worker bees do, they would go out into their fields, gather pollen from the flowers, and bring it back to make honey.

The bees had a problem, though, because every so often an intruder would come around, such as a bear who wanted the honey, or kids who thought it'd be fun to throw rocks at the hive.

Finally, the bees got tired of it. Being the intelligent bees that they are, they built an alarm system for the hive. They built it such that one bee pulls a lever, which triggers the alarm that the bees will hear from the fields, and then the bees can come back to protect their home.

There was one bee who was exclusively assigned that job, and he was aptly named the "Lever Bee." His job was to watch for potential adversaries, and pull the lever to raise the alarm.

Now obviously, the security of the hive depends on this one Lever Bee. So he has to be constantly ready and on the alert to be able to do his job.

And that, friends, is why people say, "I'm as ready as a Lever Bee."

Moral of the story: Be alert; the world needs more lerts.

MORE DAD'S COLLEGE ADVICE

A man is driving along a highway and sees a rabbit jump out across the middle of the road. He swerves to avoid hitting it, but unfortunately the rabbit jumps right in front of the car. The driver, a sensitive man as well as an animal lover, pulls over and gets out to see what has become of the rabbit. Much to his dismay, the rabbit is dead. The driver feels so awful that he begins to cry.

Another car arrives on the scene, and the driver sees the man crying on the side of the road and pulls over. She steps out of the car and asks the man what's wrong.

"I feel terrible," he explains. "I accidentally hit this rabbit and killed it."

The newcomer says, "Don't worry, I think I can help." Then she runs to her car and pulls out a spray can. She walks over to the limp, dead rabbit, bends down, and sprays the contents onto the rabbit.

Then the rabbit jumps up, waves its paw at the two of them and hops off down the road. Ten feet away the rabbit stops, turns around and waves again, he hops down the road another 10 feet, turns and waves, hops another ten feet, turns and waves, and repeats this again and again and again, until he hops out of sight.

The man is astonished. He runs over to the woman and demands, "What is in that can? What did you spray on that rabbit?"

The woman turns the can around so that the man can read the label. It says.... "Hair restorer.......adds permanent wave."

Moral of the story: When driving, watch for animals crossing the road in front of you.

MORE DAD'S COLLEGE ADVICE

For years and years, a doctor had been having a drink after work at the same bar. Every time he walked in the door, the barman would mix his favorite drink, a hazelnut daiquiri.

One day, the bartender didn't have any hazelnuts in the bar. Wondering what to do, he spied some hickory nuts and tried to make the drink from them instead.

The doctor came in at his regular time, took a sip of the drink and exclaimed, "This isn't a hazelnut daiquiri!"

"No," said the bartender, "it's a hickory daiquiri, doc."

Moral of the story: If you're going to have a drink, make sure you know who is putting what into your drink.

MORE DAD'S COLLEGE ADVICE

A law student was telling his roommate about the time he sued an airline company after it lost his luggage.

Sadly, he lost his case.

Moral of the story: Don't be lawsuit happy; sometimes accidents just happen.

MORE DAD'S COLLEGE ADVICE

Three blondes die and find themselves in front of St. Peter at the gates of Heaven. St. Peter says, "I have one question for each of you, and if you answer it correctly, I will let you into Heaven."

He starts with the first blonde and asks, "What is Easter?"

She answers, "That's the time of the year when our whole family gets together and we eat turkey."

St. Peter shakes his head no, and then asks the next blonde, "What is Easter?"

She answers, "That's the time of year when the jolly fat guy comes down the chimney and our family gets together to open presents."

Again St. Peter shakes his head, then proceeds to ask the third blonde, "What is Easter?"

She says, "That's when Christ died and they put him in a tomb behind a rock."

"That's right!" exclaims St. Peter.

"Then, once a year," continues the third blonde, "we roll the stone away and he comes out, and if he sees his shadow, we have six more weeks of winter."

Moral of the story: Pay attention in Church on Sunday; you might learn something that you'll need in order to get into heaven

MORE DAD'S COLLEGE ADVICE

There was a student returning to school after a long road trip, driving through the middle of the desert when his car broke down. He knew that he had to get back to school so he started walking, and he came to a monastery, where he asked the monks if they could help him get back to his school. The monks explained that their only mode of transportation was by mule; so the student asked if he could borrow a mule.

The monks lent him one, and they explained to him that to make the mule go you had to say "Thank the Lord!" and to make the mule stop you had to say "Amen!".

So the student thanked the monks, climbed up on the mule and said, "Thank the Lord," and the mule took off!

Now the desert was large, and the mule had been walking for a few hours, with the student dozing off, when the student was suddenly jolted awake by the sight of a huge canyon just a few yards up ahead. The student instinctively yelled "Whoa!", but the mule did not stop because that was not the correct command to make the mule stop. So it kept going, straight towards the drop-off. The student panicked trying to remember the correct phrase to make the mule stop. "Halt!" he yelled, but the mule kept advancing to the edge of the precipice.

Sweat pouring off his head, he yelled out word after word trying to get the mule to stop, all to no avail. He was coming closer and closer to the edge of the cliff and his certain doom. Finally, right at the very edge he remembered, and shouted "Amen!" and the mule stopped, one step short of tumbling down the canyon wall to certain death.

The student was so relieved, he raised his eyes to heaven and said, "Thank the Lord!"

Moral of the story: It's good to give thanks, but it's also important to follow directions.

MORE DAD'S COLLEGE ADVICE

John, a college student who was in financial difficulty, walked into a church and started to pray.

"Listen, God," John said. "I know I haven't been perfect but I really need to win the lottery. I don't have a lot of money. Please help me out."

He left the church, a week went by, and he hadn't won the lottery, so he walked into a synagogue.

"Come on, God," he said. "I really need this money. My mom needs surgery and I have student loans to pay. Please let me win the lottery."

He left the synagogue, a week went by, and he didn't win the lottery. So, he went to a mosque and started to pray again.

"You're starting to disappoint me, God," he said. "I've prayed and prayed. If you just let me win the lottery, I'll be a better person. I don't have to win the jackpot, just enough to pay off my student loans and get me out of debt. I'll give some to charity, even. Just let me win the lottery."

John thought this did it, so he got up and walked out of the mosque.

As he stepped outside, the clouds opened up and a booming voice said, "John! Buy a stinkin' lottery ticket!"

Moral of the story: God helps those who help themselves.

MORE DAD'S COLLEGE ADVICE

A Catholic priest, a Baptist preacher and a Jewish rabbi are fishing in a lake.

The preacher has to use the bathroom, so he walks across the water, does his business and walks back.

Then the rabbi has to go, so he walks across the water, does his business and walks back.

The Catholic has to go, but when he gets out he falls into the water. He swims back, gets back into the boat, and says, "God, let me walk across the water." He tries again and falls into the water, swims back, tries again and falls again.

Then the preacher leaned over to the rabbi and asked, "Do you think we should tell him where the stepping stones are?"

Moral of the story: When you see someone do something amazing, ask them how they did it; learn from the experience of others.

MORE DAD'S COLLEGE ADVICE

There's a college senior driving on the highway.

His roommate calls him on his cell phone and in a worried voice says, "Herman, be careful! I just heard on the radio that there was a madman driving the wrong way on Route 280!"

Herman says, "I know, but there isn't just one, there are hundreds!"

Moral of the story: Pay attention to which way you're going.

MORE DAD'S COLLEGE ADVICE

A student cowboy walks into a bar and orders a whiskey. Just before he takes a sip of his whiskey, a guy runs in and says, "Bill, your house burnt down!"

So he runs outside, but then he thinks, "I don't have a house," so he goes back into the bar and takes a sip of his whiskey.

Another guy runs in and says, "Bill! Your dad died!" So he runs out of the bar, gets on his horse and rides a little ways, but then thinks, "I don't have a dad," so he goes back into the bar and drinks almost all of his whiskey.

Then another guy runs in and says, "Bill! You won the lottery!" So he runs out, gets on his horse and rides all the way to the bank, but then he thinks, "My name's not Bill."

Moral of the story: Don't forget who you are or where you came from.

MORE DAD'S COLLEGE ADVICE

A student was spending his summer as a construction worker, and one day he accidentally cut off one of his ears with an electric saw.

He called out to a guy walking on the street below, "Hey, do you see my ear down there?"

The guy on the street picks up an ear and yells back, "Is this it?"

"No," replies the student construction worker. "Mine had a pencil behind it."

Moral of the story: Don't put pencils behind your ears . . . it's too easy to lose them.

MORE DAD'S COLLEGE ADVICE

A college guy burned both of his ears... so they were asking him at the hospital how it happened.

He said, "I was ironing my clothing and the phone rang. So, instead of the phone I picked up the iron and burned my ear."

"But how the heck did you burn the other ear?" the doctor asked.

"Well, whoever it was, called back."

Moral of the story is: It's okay to make mistakes, but it's a good idea to try to learn from them so that you don't repeat them.

MORE DAD'S COLLEGE ADVICE

Two student atoms are walking down the road. One exclaims, "Oh my God, I just lost an electron!"

The other atom asks, "Are you sure?"

The first atom replies, "Yes! I'm positive!"

Moral of the story: Always try to keep a positive attitude.

MORE DAD'S COLLEGE ADVICE

Three college students, turned criminals, are sentenced to exile in the desert and can only bring one personal item with them.

"I brought a loaf of bread, so when I get hungry, I'll have something to eat," said the first student turned criminal.

"I brought a water skin, so that when I get thirsty, I'll have something to drink," said the second.

The third looks proud of himself. "I brought a car door, so when it gets hot, I can roll down the window."

Moral of the story: Plan wisely, and ask for help if you're not sure.

MORE DAD'S COLLEGE ADVICE

A college student journalist went to a retirement home in order to interview an aged but legendary explorer.

The student reporter asked the old man to tell him the most frightening experience he had ever had.

The old explorer said, "Once I was hunting Bengal tigers in the jungles of India. I was on a narrow path and my faithful native gun bearer was behind me. Suddenly the largest tiger I have ever seen leapt onto the path in front of us. I turned to get my weapon only to find the native had fled. The tiger lept toward me with a mighty ROARRRR! I soiled myself."

The student reporter said, "Under those circumstances anyone would have done the same."

The old explorer replied, "No, not then . . . just now when I went 'ROARRRR!'"

Moral of the story: You can hear a lot of good stories from seniors . . . you just have to be patient in order to get the whole story.

MORE DAD'S COLLEGE ADVICE

A blonde student worker went to work in tears. Her boss asked, "What's wrong?" She said, "My mom died." The boss told her to go home, but she pulled herself together and said, "No, I'll be fine."

Later that day, her boss found her crying again. He asked, "Are you still upset about your mom?"

The blonde student replied, "No. I just talked to my sister, and her mom died, too!"

Moral of the story: Don't forget, family is always there for support when times are tough.

MORE DAD'S COLLEGE ADVICE

Two men both drag their right feet as they walk. As they meet, one man looks at the other knowingly, points to his foot and says, "Vietnam, 1969."

The other points his thumb behind him and says, "Dog poop, 20 feet back."

Moral of the story: Take care to watch where you're going so you don't end up stepping in something unpleasant.

MORE DAD'S COLLEGE ADVICE

A pastor, a doctor and an engineer are on the golf course waiting behind a particularly slow group of golfers.

The engineer fumes, "What's with these guys? We've been waiting for 15 minutes!"

The pastor says, "Hey, here comes the groundskeeper. Let's have a word with him."

"Say, George, what's with that group ahead of us? They're rather slow, aren't they?" the doctor asks.

The groundskeeper tells them that the other golfers are a group of blind firefighters who lost their sight saving the clubhouse from a fire, and that they come and play for free whenever they want. The group is silent for a moment.

The pastor says, "That's so sad. I will say a special prayer for them tonight."

The doctor says, "Good idea. I'm going to contact my ophthalmologist buddy and see if there's anything he can do for them."

The engineer says, "Why can't these guys play at night?"

Moral of the story: Don't be afraid to think outside the box.

MORE DAD'S COLLEGE ADVICE

There was once a college student, who was also a handyman. The student handyman had a dog named Mace. Mace was a great dog except he had one weird habit: he liked to eat grass – and not just a little bit, but in quantities that would make a lawnmower blush. And nothing, it seemed, could cure him of it.

One day, the student handyman lost his wrench in the tall grass while he was working outside. He looked and looked, but it was nowhere to be found. As it was getting dark, he gave up for the night and decided to look again the next morning.

When he awoke, he went outside, and saw that his dog, Mace, had eaten the all the grass in the area around where he had been working, and his wrench now lay in plain sight, glinting in the sun.

Going out to get his wrench, he called the dog over to him and said, "A grazing Mace, how sweet the hound, that saved a wrench for me."

Moral of the story: Unless you have the right kind of dog, don't set your stuff down in tall grass.

MORE DAD'S COLLEGE ADVICE

A blind college student just turned 21, so he and his Seeing Eye dog walk into a bar. After they get inside the bar, the blind student starts swinging the dog around in the air using the leash.

The bartender yells, "Yo dude! What the heck do you think you're doing!?"

The blind student says, "I ain't doing anything; I'm just looking around."

Moral of the story: Always take a look around to make sure you know where the emergency exits are located.

MORE DAD'S COLLEGE ADVICE

An Irish student walks up to a local pub, popular with many members of the local student body. As he is about to go inside he is confronted by a nun who starts shouting at him, "Before you enter this den of sin, think of your mother and your father!"

He says back to the nun, "They're deceased; they're dead and in heaven."

So the nun went for a different tactic and said, "Think then! Think of the damage the alcohol will do to your brain!"

"What?" replied the student? "Whatever are ye talking about? Have you ever had a drink yerself?" And the nun answered, "No."

"Well, how the hell can you stand there and talk about the damage the alcohol is gonna do to your brain if ye never had it yerself? I tell ye what, I'll go in there, buy ye a drink, bring it out here, then you can try it and if you don't like it, then ye can talk about it. But don't talk about things ye've never experienced. Now . . . what will ye have?"

And the nun says, "I don't know. What do ladies drink?"

"Gin," he says.

So she says, "Alright, I'll have a gin. But get it in a cup so nobody will notice."

So the fella goes into the bar and says to the barman, "Give me a pint of beer, and a double gin in a cup."

The barman replies, "Ah, fer pete's sake! Is that bloody nun out there again?"

Moral of the story: Beware of nuns, or anyone else, hanging around outside of bars.

MORE DAD'S COLLEGE ADVICE

It's business as usual for a bartender one day, as he is cleaning his bar, when an unusual customer walks in. The man is dressed in an expensive suit, has a beautiful supermodel hanging off each arm, and has a limo parked outside. But . . . the man has an orange for a head.

The customer sits down at the bar and orders everyone in the place a drink. He pays for it from a massive roll of hundreds and then manages to attract the attention of every woman in the joint, despite having an orange for a head. The bartender is not a man to pry, but he feels compelled to ask about this man's life.

"Excuse me," says the bartender, "I can't help but notice that you're obviously fabulously wealthy and irresistible to women, but you have an orange for a head. How did that happen?"

So the man told his story. "A while back, when I was penniless, I was walking along the beach and saw an old lamp, half buried in the sand. I picked it up and gave it a clean, and POOF! out popped a genie. The genie explained that he had been trapped in that lamp for two hundred years, and that he was so grateful to me for freeing him that he would give me three wishes.

"For my first wish, I asked for an unlimited fortune. The genie said 'It is done!' and from then on, whenever I needed money, it was there."

"For my second wish, I asked for the attention of all the most beautiful women in the world. The genie said it was done, and since then I have been able to get any woman I wanted. "

"For my third wish -- and, this is the bit where I kind of messed up -- I asked for an orange for a head."

Moral of the story: Don't be greedy; if someone offers you three wishes, accept two and give the third one to a friend.

MORE DAD'S COLLEGE ADVICE

A college bear walks into the cafeteria grill and says to the cook "Can I have a grilled . . . . cheese?"

The cook says to the bear, "Sure. But what's with the big pause?"

The bear replies, "Well . . . I'm a bear."

Moral of the story: When telling jokes, don't pause in the middle, because your audience won't be able to bear it.

MORE DAD'S COLLEGE ADVICE

Pony and Eagle walk up to Coyote.

Pony tells Coyote, "I am very mad at Eagle. Will you yell at him for me?"

Coyote asks, "Why can't you yell at him yourself?"

Pony replies, "Because I'm a little horse."

Moral of the story: Try not to yell at people. It's best to present your concerns in a calm manner; they'll be better received.

MORE DAD'S COLLEGE ADVICE

In the beginning was the Plan. And then came the Assumptions. And the Assumptions were without form. And the Plan was without substance. And darkness was upon the face of the Workers. And they spoke among themselves, saying, "It is a crock of s**t, and it stinketh."

And the Workers went unto their Supervisors and said, "It is a pail of dung, and none may abide the odor thereof."

And the Supervisors went unto their Managers, saying, "It is a container of excrement, and it is very strong, such that none may abide it."

And the Managers went unto their Directors, saying, "It is a vessel of fertilizer, and none may abide its strength."

And the Directors spoke amongst themselves, saying to one another, "It contains that which aids plant growth, and it is very strong."

And the Directors went unto the Vice Presidents, saying unto them, "It promotes growth, and it is very powerful."

And the Vice Presidents went unto the President, saying unto him, "This new plan will actively promote the growth and vigor of the company, with powerful effects."

And the President looked upon the Plan, and saw that it was good.

And the Plan became Policy. This is how S**t Happens.

Moral of the story: Put your grievances in writing to make sure the meaning is not lost by the time they make it to those at the top.

MORE DAD'S COLLEGE ADVICE

A man is lying sprawled across three entire seats at a posh theater before the show has even started.

A student, working as an usher, walks by, notices the man and says, "Sir, you're only allowed one seat, can you please sit up?"

The man groans, but remains lying down across the seats. The usher becomes impatient with the man, "Sir, if you don't get up, I will need to get my manager involved."

Again the man just groans, which infuriates the usher as he marches off to get the manager. In a few moments, he returns with the manager and they both repeatedly attempt to tell him to move, but with no success. It was at this point that the manager calls the police.

Moments later, a police officer arrives and approaches the man, "Alright buddy, what's your name?"

"Sam," the man moans.

"And where ya from, Sam?"

With pain in his voice Sam replies, "The balcony..."

Moral of the story: Don't judge someone's actions until you know their true motives and background.

MORE DAD'S COLLEGE ADVICE

A college student was venting to his roommate about how difficult it is for him to solve math problems that contain fractions.

"I just failed another test on fractions! It's very frustrating . . . . I think I understand it, and then still get the problem wrong. There's just a fine line between a numerator and denominator."

Moral of the story: Not all math puns are bad . . . . only sum.

MORE DAD'S COLLEGE ADVICE

A young, up-and-coming student artist was exhibiting his work for the very first time, when a world famous art critic came up and asked him, "Would you like my opinion on your work?"

"Yes!" replied the artist.

"It's worthless," said the critic.

The artist said, "Yes, I know, but tell me anyway."

Moral of the story: Opinions are like eyeballs; everybody's got them.

MORE DAD'S COLLEGE ADVICE

One morning on the way to school, a college student wasn't really paying attention and drove into the back of a car stopped at a traffic light.

The other driver got out, and it turned out he was a dwarf. He said to the student, "I'm not happy!"

The student said, "Well, which one are you then?"

Moral of the story: Not everything in the world is about that mouse company that Walt started . . . . not yet anyway . . . .

MORE DAD'S COLLEGE ADVICE

Two college roommates were talking about their families when one said, "I will always remember what my grandfather said before he kicked the bucket."

"What was it that your grandfather said?"

He said, "How far do you think I can kick this bucket?"

Moral of the story: Always keep alive the memories of those who have passed before you.

MORE DAD'S COLLEGE ADVICE

An elderly woman is driving her college student granddaughter around town, when she blows through a red light. The granddaughter doesn't want to make a scene and so she brushes it off as an honest mistake, but then her grandma drives through another red light.

So the granddaughter asks her, "Grandma, you realize you just drove through two red lights, right?"

And the grandma replies, "I'm driving?"

Moral of the story: You should offer to drive your grandparents around; it's nice, and safer that way.

MORE DAD'S COLLEGE ADVICE

A college student asked her roommate, "What rhymes with orange?"

Her roommate snapped back, "No, it doesn't!"

Moral of the story: Sometimes a question is just a question and shouldn't be used as an excuse to start an argument.

MORE DAD'S COLLEGE ADVICE

A frog goes into a bank, and hops up to the loan officer. The loan officer says, "Good morning, my name is John Paddywack. Can I help you?"

The frog says, "Yeah, I'd like to borrow some money."

The loan officer finds this a little odd, but gets out a form. He says, "Okay, what's your name?"

The frog says, "Kermit Jagger."

The loan officer says, "Really? Any relation to Mick Jagger?"

The frog says, "Yeah, he's my dad."

The loan officer says, "Okay. Ummm...do you have any collateral?"

The frog hands the loan officer a pink ceramic elephant and asks, "Will this do?"

The loan officer says, "Hmmm...I'm not sure. Let me go check with the bank manager."

The frog says, "Okay, tell him I said hi. He knows me."

The loan officer goes back to the manager and says, "Excuse me, but there's this frog out there named Kermit Jagger who wants to borrow some money. All he has for collateral is this pink elephant thing. I'm not even sure what it is."

The manager says, "It's a knick-knack, Paddywack. Give the frog a loan. His old man's a Rolling Stone."

Moral of the story: It pays to know people; build good friend networks.

MORE DAD'S COLLEGE ADVICE

A college student was complaining to his roommate about his family.

"They're always telling me to live my dreams," he grumbled.

"Well, that doesn't sound so bad," said the roommate.

"But I don't want to be naked in a classroom, taking an exam that I haven't studied for..."

Moral of the story: Make sure to schedule time to study, and set your clothes out the night before.

MORE DAD'S COLLEGE ADVICE

A grad student was talking to his classmate.

"I hired a guy to do odd jobs around the house. He was useless though. Gave him a list of eight things to do and he only did numbers one, three, five and seven."

Moral of the story: Get your business agreements in writing before exchanging any money.

MORE DAD'S COLLEGE ADVICE

A college student told her roommate, "I needed a password eight characters long, so I picked Snow White and the Seven Dwarfs."

Moral of the story: Choose good passwords and just another reminder that not everything is about that mouse company that Walt started . . . . not yet anyway.

MORE DAD'S COLLEGE ADVICE

Two college roommates were sharing stories about what they had done over break.

One said, "I was watching the Boston Marathon and saw one runner dressed as a chicken and another runner dressed as an egg. And I thought: 'This could be interesting.'"

Moral of the story: Take time to ponder the great philosophical questions of life.

MORE DAD'S COLLEGE ADVICE

A college student was telling his roommate about advice he'd received from his father.

"My dad said, always leave them wanting more. Ironically, that's how he lost his job in disaster relief."

Moral of the story: When deciding whether or not to make a purchase, ask yourself, "Do I need this, or do I want this?"

MORE DAD'S COLLEGE ADVICE

A college student was complaining to his roommate about getting spam calls on his phone.

"I called up my phone service provider, and I said to the guy, 'I want to report a nuisance caller', and the guy said 'Not you again.'"

Moral of the story: Don't be a chronic complainer; people will start to tune out even your legitimate complaints.

MORE DAD'S COLLEGE ADVICE

Two college students were talking about their experiences growing up.

The one said, "I could tell my parents hated me. My bath toys were a toaster and a radio."

Moral of the story: Be thankful for what you've got because sometimes having no toys at all is a better option.

MORE DAD'S COLLEGE ADVICE

Two college students were commiserating with each other.

The first one said, "You know . . . it's times like this that make me wish I had listened to what my mother always told me."

"And what was it that she said?" asked the other.

The first one answered, "I don't know. I was never listening."

Moral of the story: Always listen to your mother.

MORE DAD'S COLLEGE ADVICE

Some college students were relaxing at the local coffee shop.

One of them took a sip of his coffee and said, "I was sitting in traffic the other day. That's probably why I got run over."

Moral of the story: Obey traffic laws, and don't play in traffic.

MORE DAD'S COLLEGE ADVICE

Two college students were chatting one day.

One said, "Sometimes I tuck my knees into my chest and lean forward."

"Why?" asked the other.

"That's just how I roll."

Moral of the story: Sometimes you just have to roll with the punches.

MORE DAD'S COLLEGE ADVICE

Two college students were conversing about life and mysteries of the universe when one asked, "Why are hamsters like cigarettes?"

His friend answered, "Because they're both completely harmless until you put one in your mouth and light it on fire."

Moral of the story: Don't smoke, cigarettes or hamsters; they're bad for you, and for those around you.

MORE DAD'S COLLEGE ADVICE

Two English university students are sitting on the deck of a cruise ship.

The first one asks, "Have you read Marx?"

The other one replies, "Yes. I believe that comes from sitting on these wicker chairs."

Moral of the story: The vast majority of buttocks are overused, whereas the majority of minds are underused; choose wisely which one you will use the most.

MORE DAD'S COLLEGE ADVICE

A college student told his roommate, "I had to give up my vegetarian diet."

"Why is that?" asked his roommate.

He answered, "Turns out they're a lot harder to catch than cows."

Moral of the story: Eat right; a good diet makes it easier to get good grades.

MORE DAD'S COLLEGE ADVICE

A college student was talking to her classmates, trying to put a positive spin on the obscure terms their professor expected the class to know.

She said to them, "The word 'diputseromneve' may look ridiculous...but backwards it's 'even more stupid'."

Moral of the story: To make sure you do well on finals, study until you know the material frontwards and backwards.

MORE DAD'S COLLEGE ADVICE

A college student walks into the doctor's office with a big white duck on his head.

The doctor looks up and says, "Yes, can I help you?"

The duck says, "Yeah, can you get this guy off my butt?"

Moral of the story: Those with different perspectives of a problem and opposing viewpoints of how it should be solved often want the same end result but just don't realize it.

MORE DAD'S COLLEGE ADVICE

Two college students were up late one night talking about their families.

One said to the other, "My grandfather is always saying that back in the old days people could leave their back doors open . . . "

"Which is probably why his submarine sank..."

Moral of the story: Keep yourself safe; lock things up at night. And make sure you have your keys with you before going out the door.

MORE DAD'S COLLEGE ADVICE

A college student in a taxi wanted to speak to the driver, so he leaned forward and tapped the driver on the shoulder. The driver screamed in fright, jumped up in the air and yanked the wheel over. The car mounted the curb, demolished a lamppost and came to a stop inches from a shop window.

The startled passenger said, "I'm sorry! I really didn't mean to frighten you. I just wanted to ask you something."

The taxi driver said, "It's ok, it's not your fault. You see, this is my first day as a cab driver. I've been driving a hearse for the past 25 years!"

Moral of the story: Be patient with newbies, whether it's yourself or someone else; it takes time to adjust to new situations.

MORE DAD'S COLLEGE ADVICE

Two college students were taking a break from studying for finals when the first said to the second, "Would you like to hear a really good Batman impression?"

The second one said, "Sure. Go for it."

So the first student got up, struck a dramatic pose, and screamed in a loud voice, "Oh no! Not the kryptonite!"

The second stared at him, dumbfounded, and said, "That's Superman."

Sitting back down, the first replied, "Thanks dude! I've been practicing a lot."

Moral of the story: Make sure you study the correct material for each exam.

MORE DAD'S COLLEGE ADVICE

A college student was telling his roommate about a trip he took to the beach, with his father, when he was four years old.

"There was a dead seagull lying on the sand, so I asked my father, 'Dad, what happened to the birdie?'"

"Dad told me, 'Son, the bird died and went to heaven.'"

"So I asked, 'Did God throw him back down?'"

Moral of the story: Always be a good person; you don't want God throwing you back down.

MORE DAD'S COLLEGE ADVICE

A college student was helping his roommate prepare for finals by quizzing him . . . .

Q: There are 500 bricks on a plane. One falls off. How many are left?
A: 499

Q: What are the 3 steps needed to put an elephant into a refrigerator?
A: 1- open fridge, 2- put elephant in, 3- close fridge

Q: What are the 4 steps needed to put a giraffe into a refrigerator?
A: 1- open fridge, 2- take elephant out, 3- put giraffe in, 4- close fridge

Q: The lion king is having a birthday party. All the animals show up but one. Which animal is the no-show?
A: The giraffe, because he's stuck in a refrigerator

Q: Sally wants to cross a river known to be infested with man-eating crocodiles. There is no bridge. The only way she can get across is by swimming. So she decides to swims across, and she makes it across without getting eaten by crocodiles. Why didn't she get eaten?
A: All the crocodiles were at the birthday party

Q: Sally dies anyway. Why?
A: She got hit in the head with a falling brick

Moral of the story: The buddy system is beneficial when swimming and studying; but choose your buddy wisely.

MORE DAD'S COLLEGE ADVICE

Two college students were in a coffee shop complaining about their respective roommates.

The first one said, "I am so mad at my roommate. He keeps treating me like I'm a little kid or something. Like just last night he told me that I was immature and that I needed to grow up."

"Wow. So what did you do? " his friend asked.

"I told him to get out of my fort."

Moral of the story: Be open to constructive criticism; you don't always need to take it personally.

MORE DAD'S COLLEGE ADVICE

A college student, who happened to be a cowboy, rode into town and stopped at a saloon for a drink. Unfortunately, the locals always had a habit of picking on strangers, which he was.

When he finished his drink, he found his horse had been stolen. He went back into the bar, handily flipped his gun into the air, caught it above his head without even looking and fired a shot into the ceiling. "Which one of you sidewinders stole my horse?!?!?" he yelled with surprising forcefulness.

No one answered.

"Alright, I'm gonna have another beer, and if my horse ain't back outside by the time I finish, I'm gonna do what I dun in Texas! And I don't like to have to do what I dun in Texas!"

Some of the locals shifted restlessly. The man, true to his word, had another beer, walked outside, and his horse had been returned to the post. He saddled up and started to ride out of town.

The bartender wandered out of the bar and asked, "Say partner, before you go... what happened in Texas?"

The cowboy turned back and said, "I had to walk home."

Moral of the story: Always exuding self-confidence will persuade more people to your point of view.

MORE DAD'S COLLEGE ADVICE

Three blonde college students were walking in the countryside one day. They saw a set of tracks and started arguing over what kind of tracks they were.

The first blonde said, "I think they're deer tracks!"

The second blonde said, "I think they're dog tracks!"

The third blonde said, "Well, I think they're cow tracks!"

They were still arguing when the train hit them.

Moral of the story: Arguing about something you know nothing about is foolish; and don't play on train tracks.

MORE DAD'S COLLEGE ADVICE

A drunk college student decides to go ice fishing, so he drills a hole in the ice and peers into it. As he does so, a loud voice from above says, "There are no fish down there."

So the drunk college student fisherman walks several yards away and drills another hole. As he peers into it he again hears a voice say, "There are no fish down there."

So he walks about 20 yards away and drills another hole. Once again the voice says, "There are no fish down there."

The college student fisherman looks up to the sky and asks, "God, is that you?"

"No, you idiot," says the voice. "It's the rink manager."

Moral of the story: Don't fish at ice rinks, you might end up in the penalty box.

MORE DAD'S COLLEGE ADVICE

Three college students were driving down a lonely country road one night. Suddenly, the car broke down. One student was a mechanic, but try as he might, he couldn't get the car to start. They checked, but there was no cell phone reception for at least a hundred yards in every direction. Looking around, they saw a dim light far in the distance, and with no other option, they headed towards it.

About halfway there, the wind was becoming fierce. A storm was brewing. They had a brief debate on whether or not to go back to the car, but decided if they were to go back, the wind would be against them, and so continued on. As the rain started to come down, they found the light was from a bed and breakfast.

The proprietor was a skinny old woman, so deaf that the students needed to shout to get her attention, but polite enough, and was not at all unhappy about them checking in so late. They decided that since it was late, so they would call a tow truck in the morning, and went to bed.

They woke up the next morning and went downstairs for breakfast. The first student ordered Corn Flakes, the second student ordered Corn Flakes, and the third student ordered Fruit Loops.

Moral of the story: Two out of three students choose Corn Flakes; and it's okay if you don't.

MORE DAD'S COLLEGE ADVICE

A college student, who happened to be a horse, limps into a bar one day. He's got a bandage around his head and looks really ill. He orders a glass of the most expensive champagne, a vintage brandy and two pints of Guinness.

When the bartender serves them to him, he quickly downs them all. Then he says, "You know, I shouldn't really be drinking this with what I've got..."

The bartender asks, "Why, what have you got?"

The horse replies, "About 2 dollars and a carrot."

Moral of the story: Don't buy things unless you have the cash to pay for them; use credit only as a last resort, in the case of true emergencies.

MORE DAD'S COLLEGE ADVICE

Two college students were in a coffee shop talking about their grandparents.

The first one said, "My grandmother walks for her health. She started walking five miles a day when she was 60. She's 97 today and we don't know where she is."

Moral of the story: Exercise regularly, preferably with a workout buddy who will help keep you on track for achieving your fitness goals.

MORE DAD'S COLLEGE ADVICE

Two college students were in a coffee shop talking.

The first one said, "I hate it when people don't know the difference between your and you're. There so stupid."

"Aye no, write?" replied his friend.

Moral of the story: Don't judge and condemn actions of others, especially when you may be guilty of the same offenses.

MORE DAD'S COLLEGE ADVICE

Two college students were in a coffee shop talking about people back home.

The first one said, "I had a friend who was a clown. When he died, all his friends went to the funeral in one car."

Moral of the story: Carpooling is good.

MORE DAD'S COLLEGE ADVICE

Two college students were in a coffee shop talking about their life experiences.

The first one said, "I once had some eyeglasses. I was walking down the street with them one day when suddenly the prescription ran out."

Moral of the story: Plan ahead for expiration dates and deadlines.

MORE DAD'S COLLEGE ADVICE

Two college students were in a coffee shop complaining about their respective roommates.

The first one said, "My roommate is insane. The guy designs synthetic hairballs for ceramic cats."

"That's nothing," countered the second student. "My roommate tried to rob a department store...with a pricing gun...he told them, 'Give me all of the money in the vault, or I'm marking down everything in the store.'"

Moral of the story: Good roommates are priceless; make sure they know that you appreciate them.

MORE DAD'S COLLEGE ADVICE

Two college students were in a coffee shop comparing notes on local restaurants.

The first said, "I went to a restaurant that serves 'breakfast at any time'. So I ordered French Toast during the Renaissance."

Moral of the story: Pay attention to the expiration dates on your food.

MORE DAD'S COLLEGE ADVICE

A college student is giving a friend a tour of his new apartment, as they take a break from an all-night study session. The last stop is the bedroom, where a big brass gong sits next to the bed.

"What's that gong for?" the friend asks him.

"It's not a gong," the student replies.   "It's a talking clock."

"No kidding! How does it work?"

The student picks up a hammer, gives the gong an ear-shattering pound, and steps back.

Suddenly, someone on the other side of the wall screams, "For God's sake, you idiot! It's 3:30 in the morning!"

Moral of the story: Good neighbors are worth their weight in gold; don't unnecessarily annoy them.

MORE DAD'S COLLEGE ADVICE

Three students, a blonde, a brunette, and a redhead, are crossing an enchanted bridge in Magical University Fairyland when they run into a fairy. The fairy says that they can be granted a transformation if they jump off the bridge and call out their wish.

The brunette thinks for a moment then jumps off the bridge and yells "Eagle!" She turns into a beautiful bird of prey and flies away.

The redhead contemplates her wish then jumps off the bridge and yells out "Salmon!" She turns into a gorgeous shimmering salmon and swims upstream to spawn.

The blonde sees all this and gets so excited that she jumps off the bridge without thinking of her wish. Not knowing what to wish for, she exclaims, "Rat farts!"

Moral of the story: Fools rush in; think before you act.

MORE DAD'S COLLEGE ADVICE

"The 24th of December is Christmas Eve."

"No it isn't, Adam."

Moral of the story: People have been having disagreements since the beginning of time; the key is to disagree amicably.

MORE DAD'S COLLEGE ADVICE

Two college students were talking over coffee one day.

The first said, "I asked my girlfriend what she wanted for Christmas. She told me 'Nothing would make me happier than a diamond necklace.' So I bought her nothing."

Moral of the story: It's always better to give than to receive.

MORE DAD'S COLLEGE ADVICE

There was a college student who absolutely loved hollandaise sauce. He would buy the sharpest brand he could find and would put it on just about everything. Well, it turned out that because he used the spicy sauce so much, it started to wear a hole in the roof of his mouth.

He went to a doctor and asked what he could do about it. The doctor looked at the damage and determined that the student would need a metal plate placed in the roof of his mouth.

The student was somewhat relieved but couldn't help asking the doctor if he would still be able to enjoy his hollandaise sauce. The doctor reassured the student, telling him that his new plate would be made of chrome. The student was curious, so he asked if chrome was the best choice.

The doctor responded, "Oh don't worry, there's no plate like chrome for the hollandaise."

Moral of the story: There really is no place like home for the holidays.

MORE DAD'S COLLEGE ADVICE

A college student asked his roommate what he had done over the holidays.

The roommate answered, "Well, a couple of nights ago, I was out for a few drinks with some friends and had a few too many beers, and some rather nice chardonnay."

He continued, "Knowing full well I may have been slightly over the limit, I did something I've never done before – I took a bus home. I arrived home safely and without incident, which was a real surprise, because I had never driven a bus before and I'm not even sure where I got it."

Moral of the story: Never go to excess, but let moderation be your guide.

MORE DAD'S COLLEGE ADVICE

This college student goes into a doctor's office all cut up and bruised and the doctor says, "My goodness, what happened to you?"

The student says, "Well I was in this horse race and I fell off my horse. And then the horse started jumping up and down on top of me."

And the doctor says, "That must have been terrible!"

The student replies, "I know. I would have been killed if the Wal-Mart man hadn't unplugged the machine."

Moral of the story: Be kind to animals, even if you will eventually be eating them.

MORE DAD'S COLLEGE ADVICE

A college student was driving through west Texas one spring evening. The road was deserted and he had not seen a soul for what seemed like hours. Suddenly his car started to cough and splutter and the engine slowly died, leaving him sitting on the side of the road in total isolation. He popped the hood and looked to see if there was anything that he could do to get it going again. Unfortunately, he had a limited knowledge of cars, so all he could do was look at the engine and feel despondent. As he stood looking at the gradually fading light of his flashlight, he cursed that he had not put in new batteries. Suddenly, through the inky shadows, came a deep voice, "It's your fuel pump." The student raised up quickly, striking his head on the underside of the hood.

"Who said that?" he called out. There were two horses, a white one and a black one, standing in the fenced field alongside the road.

The student was amazed when the white horse repeated, "It's your fuel pump. Tap it with your flashlight and try it again." Confused, the student tapped the fuel pump with his flashlight, turned the key and sure enough, the engine roared to life. He muttered a short thanks to the horse and screeched away. When he reached the next town, he ran into the local bar. "Gimme a large whiskey, please!" he said.

A rancher sitting at the bar looked at the student's ashen face and asked, "What's wrong? You look like you've seen a ghost."

"Well, you're not gonna believe this," the student said and then recounted the whole tale to the rancher. The rancher took a sip of his beer and looked thoughtful. "A horse, you say? Was it by any chance a white horse?" The student replied to the affirmative. "Yes, it was! Am I crazy?"

"No, you ain't crazy. In fact, you're lucky," said the rancher, "because that black horse don't know crap about cars."

Moral of the story: Find a good mechanic that you trust; they are worth their weight in gold.

MORE DAD'S COLLEGE ADVICE

One sunny day, a rabbit college student came out of her hole in the ground to enjoy the weather. The day was so nice that the rabbit became careless, so a fox sneaked up on her and caught her. "I am going to eat you for lunch!" said the fox.

"Wait!" replied the rabbit. "You should at least wait a few days."

"Oh yeah? Why should I wait?"

"Well, I am just finishing writing my Ph.D. thesis."

"Hah! That's a stupid excuse. What's the title of this thesis you claim to be writing?"

"I am writing my thesis on 'The Superiority of Rabbits over Foxes and Wolves'."

"Are you crazy? I should eat you up right now! Everybody knows that a fox will always win over a rabbit!"

"Not really, not according to my research. If you like, you can come to my hole and read it for yourself. If you are not convinced, you can go ahead and have me for lunch."

"You really are crazy!" But, since the fox was curious and had nothing to lose, it went with the rabbit into its hole. The fox never came back out.

A few days later, the rabbit was again taking a break from writing and, sure enough, a wolf came out of the bushes and was ready to eat her. "Wait!" yelled the rabbit. "You cannot eat me right now."

"And why might that be, you fuzzy appetizer?" asked the wolf.

"I am almost finished writing my Ph.D. thesis on 'The Superiority of Rabbits over Foxes and Wolves'."

The wolf laughed so hard that it almost lost its hold on the rabbit. "Maybe I shouldn't eat you; you really are sick in your head, and you might have something contagious," the wolf opined.

"Come read my thesis for yourself. You can eat me after that if you disagree with my conclusions." So the wolf went to the rabbit's hole, and never came out again.

The rabbit finished writing her thesis and was out celebrating in the lettuce fields. Another rabbit came by and asked, "What's up with you? You seem very happy."

"Yup, I just finished writing my dissertation."

"Congratulations! What is it about?"

"It is titled 'The Superiority of Rabbits over Foxes and Wolves'."

"Are you sure? That doesn't sound right."

"Oh yes, you should come over and read it for yourself." So they went together to the rabbit's hole.

As they went in, the friend saw the typical graduate-student abode, albeit a rather messy one after writing a thesis. The computer with the controversial dissertation was in one corner. On the right there was a pile of fox bones, on the left there was a pile of wolf bones, and in the middle was a gigantic lion.

Moral of the story: Get to know your professors and advisors, because the title of your dissertation doesn't matter; the quality of the research doesn't matter; all that really matters is who your thesis advisor is.

MORE DAD'S COLLEGE ADVICE

A conversation in a classroom one day went like this:

Teacher: Tell me a sentence that starts with an 'I'.

Student: I is the....

Teacher: Stop! Never put 'is' after an 'I'. Always put 'am' after an 'I'.

Student: OK. I am the ninth letter of the alphabet.

Moral of the story: Don't assume that you know what someone is going to say; let them finish, then you'll know for sure.

MORE DAD'S COLLEGE ADVICE

Some college students had formed a book club and were discussing their favorite books.

One student said, "I love Harry Potter, but after re-reading the chapter with the Death-Day party I realized something about Nearly Headless Nick."

"What?" asked another.

"He was a very poorly executed character."

Moral of the story: Take your time to try and do things right; and if you don't succeed the first time . . . take note of what you've learned and try again. In life you learn more from failures than from successes.

MORE DAD'S COLLEGE ADVICE

A college student came back to his dorm room to find his roommate holding an ice pack on his face and moaning in pain.

"What happened to you," he asked?

His roommate replied, "Well . . . I was walking past the mental hospital, and all the patients were shouting '13...13...13'."

He continued, "The fence was too high to see over, but I saw a little gap in the planks, so I looked through the hole to see what was going on." Then he sat silently for a moment, sniffling.

"Well? What did you see?" the first student asked.

"Nothing! Some idiot poked me in the eye with a stick, and then they all started shouting '14...14...14'."

Moral of the story: Some questions are best left unanswered.

MORE DAD'S COLLEGE ADVICE

Two college students were having a late night coffee.

One said to the other, "If you stand by the sea, it sounds like putting a shell to your ear."

Moral of the story: Take time to look at things from different perspectives.

MORE DAD'S COLLEGE ADVICE

A college student approached his professor and said, "Sorry professor, I won't be coming to class for the big exam."

"Why's that?" said the professor.

"Yes, very wise indeed," replied the student.

Moral of the story: Be prepared for unanticipated absences, and don't assume others agree with or understand your reasoning for being absent.

MORE DAD'S COLLEGE ADVICE

Two college student nerds were taking a break from debating which comic universe was better, Marvel or DC.

"How are you and your girlfriend getting along?" asked the first.

"Not too good, I think," replied his friend.

"Why do you think that?"

"Well, the other night we were having an argument about what movie to watch. She wanted to watch a chick flick, but I wanted to watch Justice League. She came right out and told me that she was angry with me."

"Whoa, dude. What did you do?"

"I grabbed a towel, draped it around her shoulders, and shouted out that now she was 'Super Angry'."

Moral of the story: Take time to learn about the interests of others; it'll broaden your horizons and you might just find something new that you enjoy.

MORE DAD'S COLLEGE ADVICE

A college student accompanied his roommate on a visit to his doctor, when his roommate returned to the waiting room with a shocked look on his face.

"What's wrong? What did the doctor say?" the roommate asked.

"He diagnosed me with color blindness . . . it came completely out of the purple."

Moral of the story: Don't assume that the way you see things is the only way to see things.

MORE DAD'S COLLEGE ADVICE

Some college students were hanging out in their dorm lobby waiting for their RA to start a floor meeting.

One student turns to the guy next to him and asks, "Do you know the difference between toilet paper and a shower curtain?"

"No...," replied the second student.

Then the first student shouted out, "Cancel the meeting, everybody! I found the guy!"

Moral of the story: Use the proper tool for the proper job, but if you have to improvise, then for Pete's sake, clean up afterward.

MORE DAD'S COLLEGE ADVICE

A student is driving around town with a car full of penguins. He gets pulled over and the officer tells him that he needs to take those penguins to the zoo.

The next day the student is driving with his penguins again and is pulled over by the same officer. The officer looks at the student and says, "Son, didn't I tell you to take those penguins to the zoo?"

"Yes, Officer you did, and today I'm taking them to the movies."

Moral of the story: Always follow directions, but first make sure you understand the directions.

MORE DAD'S COLLEGE ADVICE

Two college students were chatting one day about the people in their families.

"My uncle fell off a scaffolding and was killed," said the first.

"Wow, that's too bad," replied his friend. "What was he doing up on the scaffolding?"

"Getting hanged," answered the first.

Moral of the story: People are often judged by the company they keep, so choose carefully those with whom you hang.

MORE DAD'S COLLEGE ADVICE

An arrogant professor boards a plane and gets a seat besides an old man.

Mid-flight, the professor decides to humiliate the old man and prove he's intellectually superior, so he turns to him and says, "Hey, do you want to play a little game with me?"

The old man eyes him warily and says, "Depends. What type of game?"

The professor goes on to explain the game: "Taking turns, we'll ask each other one question at a time. If the other knows the answer, the asker gives him one dollar, and if he doesn't, he gives one dollar to the asker. Want to play?"

The professor grins, knowing his general knowledge is vastly superior to that of the old man.

To his dismay, the old man refuses!

Determined to make him agree, the professor raises the stakes for him. "If I lose, I'll give you two dollars instead of one!"

"No."

"Five dollars!"

"No."

"Ten dollars!"

"I told you, no."

Desperate, the professor makes one final offer. "If I lose, I'll give you a hundred dollars, and if you lose, you'll only give me one!" the professor pleads.

The old man ponders this, then sighs, "Only if I get to start," and the professor immediately agrees.

"Ask away," the professor says, confident he'll never lose.

The old man asks, "What has five heads, forty feet and lives inside of a bucket?"

The professor turns the riddle over in his head, trying to find anything that fits the description. After an hour of intense concentration, the professor gives up.

Grumbling, he pulls out his wallet and gives the old man $100. He wastes no time and asks the old man, "So what has five heads, forty feet and lives inside of a bucket?"

The old man smiles, shrugs and says, "I've got no idea. Here's your dollar."

Moral of the story: Just because you know a lot of stuff, it doesn't mean that you are smart.

MORE DAD'S COLLEGE ADVICE

It's the day of Jesus' crucifixion, and John the Apostle is having an especially hard time. John loves Jesus more than anything, and he can't bear the thought of him dying, so he doesn't go to the crucifixion.

Unfortunately, John's house directly overlooks the hill on which Jesus is being crucified. So John is pacing around his house, trying to distract himself, when he hears a faint "Johhhhhn, Johhhhhhhhn" from the hill - it's Jesus calling him.

So John runs out of his house to the hill, where several Roman centurions are keeping guard. When the guards stop him, John explains, "Jesus has a message for me. I need to go up there."

The centurions deny him, and one of them whacks him with the hilt of his sword. Defeated, John returns to his house and resumes his activities, trying to forget what has happened. But about an hour later, John hears it again, only louder this time - "Johhhhhhhhn! Jooooohhhhhhhhhhhnnnnn!"

John is kicking himself for trying to ignore the call of Jesus, and he returns to the hill, this time even more determined to hear Jesus' message.

Knowing that the centurions will try to stop him again, he sprints towards them, taking one of them down with a flying tackle. Still, the centurions are able to apprehend him as he shouts, "Jesus has an important message for me! Let me hear the dying words of my Lord!"

The centurions proceed to beat the hell out of him and toss him down the hill. John returns home to tend to his wounds and pray to God for forgiveness for failing to be at Jesus' side as he dies.

Then, clearer and louder than ever, he hears it again. "JOOOOHHHHHHHHHHN!
JOOOOOOOOOOHHHHHHHHNNNN!!!"

To hell with it, John thinks, I've got to get up there, even if those centurions kill me.

So John comes running out of his house once more, this time with a ladder. He runs up the hill, whacking all the centurions with the ladder and sending them tumbling down the hill.

John finally reaches Jesus' cross at the top of the hill and begins to climb the ladder up to him. The centurions make it up there as he's climbing and begin breaking apart the ladder with their swords.

John knows he's a dead man, but nothing will stop him from hearing Jesus' final message.

He reaches the top of the ladder and gets up close to Jesus' ear and says, "Jesus, I'm here. What is your message?"

Jesus turns his head with a pained look in his eyes, and says through labored breaths, "John ... I can see your house from here!"

Moral of the story: Be a good friend, especially when things are at their darkest.

MORE DAD'S COLLEGE ADVICE

Two college students and their professor are walking to lunch when they find an antique oil lamp. They rub it and a Genie comes out.

The Genie says, "I'll give each of you just one wish."

"Me first! Me first!" says the first student. "I want to be in the Bahamas, driving a speedboat, without a care in the world."

And poof! She's gone.

"Me next! Me next!" says the second student. "I want to be in Hawaii, relaxing on the beach with my personal masseuse, an endless supply of Pina Coladas and the love of my life."

Then poof! He's also gone.

"OK, you're up," the Genie says to the professor.

The professor says, "I want those two back in class right after lunch."

Moral of the story: Always let your professor have the first say.

MORE DAD'S COLLEGE ADVICE

A man and wife are in bed sleeping when they hear a knocking on the door. The man rolls over and looks at his clock, and it's half past three in the morning.

"I'm not getting out of bed at this time," he thinks, and rolls over.

Then, a louder knock follows. "Aren't you going to answer that?" says his wife.

So he drags himself out of bed and goes downstairs. He opens the door, and there is a man standing at the door. It didn't take the homeowner long to realize the man was drunk.

"Hi there," slurs the stranger. "Can you give me a push?"

"No, get lost. It's half past three. I was in bed," says the man and slams the door.

He goes back up to bed and tells his wife what happened and she says, "Dave, that wasn't very nice of you. Remember that night we broke down in the pouring rain on the way to pick the kids up from the baby sitter and you had to knock on that man's house to get us started again? What would have happened if he'd told us to get lost??"

"But the guy was drunk," says the husband.

"It doesn't matter," says the wife. "He needs our help and it would be the right thing to help him."

So the husband gets out of bed again, gets dressed, and goes downstairs.

He opens the door, and not being able to see the stranger anywhere he shouts out, "Hey, do you still want a push??"

Dad's College Advice

And he hears a voice cry out, "Yes please."

So, still being unable to see the stranger he shouts, "Where are you?"

And the stranger replies, "I'm over here. On your swing."

Moral of the story: Be ready to help those who ask, but sometimes it's wise to make sure they really need the kind of help that they are asking for.

MORE DAD'S COLLEGE ADVICE

A college student was driving home when he saw flashing lights in his rear view mirror. He pulled over to the side of the road, rolled down his window and then waited as the police officer got out of his patrol car.

The officer approached the student's car, looked at the student, and in an authoritative tone of voice said, "Papers."

The student replied, "Scissors. I win." And then drove off.

Moral of the story: Drive safely, and don't ever try this at home (or away from home).

MORE DAD'S COLLEGE ADVICE

A college student asked his roommate where he had been all night.

"Well," his roommate replied, "I was out walking last night, and I decided to take a short cut through a Cemetery when three girls came towards me and said they were petrified walking through the grave yard. They asked if they could walk alongside me, so I said yes."

"As we were walking, I said, 'don't worry. I understand. I used to be petrified walking through here too . . . . . . when I was alive.'...Never seen anybody run so fast."

Moral of the story: Everyone has their fears, and eventually they have to face them; find a good support network and face them head on.

MORE DAD'S COLLEGE ADVICE

Two students were trying to warm up with hot cups of coffee on a cold winter morning.

The first one said, "Is something wrong? You look terrible this morning."

"Well, I didn't sleep too well last night," replied the second. "It was so cold that I decided to try out my new electric blanket. But I accidentally plugged it into my toaster and kept popping out of bed all night."

Moral of the story: On frigid days it's best to dress in several thin layers; remember that warm hats and gloves are your friends; expose as little skin as possible to the wind and cold.

MORE DAD'S COLLEGE ADVICE

The Indians asked their Chief, in autumn, if the winter was going to be cold or not.

Not really knowing the answer, the chief replies that the winter was going to be cold and that the members of the village were to collect wood to be prepared.

Being a good leader, he then went to the next room and called the National Weather Service and asked, "Is this winter to be cold?"

The man on the phone responded, "This winter is going to be quite cold indeed." So the Chief went back to speed up his people to collect even more wood to be prepared.

A week later he called the National Weather Service again, "Is it going to be a very cold winter?"

"Yes", the man replied, "it's going to be a very cold winter." So the Chief goes back to his people and orders them to go and find every scrap of wood they can find.

Two weeks later he calls the National Weather Service again. "Are you absolutely sure that the winter is going to be very cold?"

"Absolutely," the man replies, "the Indians are collecting wood like crazy."

Moral of the story: Weathermen, Indians, woolly caterpillars, or dice, take your pick, but always be prepared for the weather.

MORE DAD'S COLLEGE ADVICE

Two Jesuit novices both wanted a cigarette while they prayed. They decided to ask their superior for permission.

The first asked but was told no. But a little while later he spotted his friend smoking and praying.

"Why did the superior allow you to smoke and not me?" he asked.

His friend replied, "Because you asked if you could smoke while you prayed, and I asked if I could pray while I smoked."

Moral of the story: When asking for something, how you ask is just as important as what you are asking for.

MORE DAD'S COLLEGE ADVICE

A college student from Boston was visiting home and talking with his father.

"Dad," he said, "how do you win a Superbowl without cheating?"

"I don't know son; we're Patrlots fans."

Moral of the story: Don't be dishonest; it's difficult to gain back someone's trust once you've betrayed it.

MORE DAD'S COLLEGE ADVICE

A Saints fan, a Chiefs fan, a Rams fan, and a Patriots fan are climbing a mountain and arguing about who loves his team more.

The Patriots fan insists he is the most loyal. "This is for the Patriots!" he yells, and jumps off the side of the mountain.

Not to be outdone, the Chiefs fan shouts, "This is for the Chiefs!" and throws himself off the mountain.

The Saints fan is next to profess his love for his team. He yells, "This is for everyone!" and throws the Rams fan off the mountain.

Moral of the story: Loyalty is good, but don't be blindly loyal.

MORE DAD'S COLLEGE ADVICE

Two college roommates were talking over lunch one day.

The first one said, "What has 4 letters, sometimes has 9 letters, but never has 5 letters."

Moral of the story: When writing papers, pay attention to punctuation, as it can drastically change the meaning of a sentence.

MORE DAD'S COLLEGE ADVICE

A blonde student was desperate for money. So she decided to go to the richer neighborhoods around town and look for odd jobs.

At the first house, a man answered the door and told her, "Yeah, I have a job for you. Could you paint the porch?"

"Sure," smiled the blonde student. "I'll do it for $100."

"Great," the man replied. "You'll find the paint and stuff you need in the garage."

The man went back into the house to his wife, who'd been listening. "A hundred bucks! Does she know it goes all the way around the house?" asked the wife.

"Well, she must. She was standing right on it!" he said.

About 45 minutes later, the blonde knocked on the door. "I'm all done," she reported.

The man was amazed. "You painted the whole porch?"

"Yep," the blonde student replied. "I even had enough paint to put on two coats!"

The man reached into his wallet to pay her.

"And by the way," said the blonde student, "that's not a Porsche. It's a Ferrari."

Moral of the story: Make sure both parties clearly understand what is expected of them before agreeing to make a deal.

MORE DAD'S COLLEGE ADVICE

An eccentric philosophy professor gave a one question final exam after a whole semester dealing with a broad array of topics.

The class was already seated and ready to go when the professor picked up his chair, plopped it on his desk and wrote on the board, "Using everything we have learned this semester, prove that this chair does not exist."

Fingers flew, erasers erased, notebooks were filled in furious fashion. Some students wrote over 30 pages in one hour attempting to refute the existence of the chair.

One member of the class however, was up and finished in less than a minute.

Weeks later when the grades were posted, the rest of the group wondered how he could have gotten an "A" when he had barely written anything at all.

His answer consisted of two words: "What chair?"

Moral of the story: Try not to overcomplicate things; many times a simple and direct solution is all that is needed.

MORE DAD'S COLLEGE ADVICE

Two students were hanging out in the cafeteria doing crossword puzzles.

"Hey, what's the opposite of irony?" asked the first.

"Wrinkly," replied the other.

Moral of the story: Dress nicely and neatly when interviewing for jobs and internships.

MORE DAD'S COLLEGE ADVICE

Two college students flew to Canada on a hunting trip. They chartered a small plane to take them into the Rockies for a week hunting moose. They managed to bag six moose.

As they were loading the plane to return, the Pilot said the plane could take only 4 moose.

The two students objected strongly. "Last year we shot six. The pilot let us take them all and he had the same plane as yours."

Reluctantly, the pilot gave in and all six moose were loaded.

The plane took off. However, while attempting to cross some mountains, even on full power, the little plane couldn't handle the load; it went down and crashed.

Surrounded by the moose bodies, only the two students survived the crash.

After climbing out of the wreckage, the first one asked, "Any idea where we are?"

The second replied, "I think we're pretty close to where we crashed last year."

Moral of the story: Learn from your mistakes and adjust; the definition of insanity is doing the same thing over and over again and expecting a different result.

MORE DAD'S COLLEGE ADVICE

A college student was talking to a classmate over a cup of coffee.

He said, "Last year I entered a marathon. The race started and immediately I was the last of the runners. It was embarrassing."

"The guy who was in front of me, second to last, was making fun of me. He said, 'Hey buddy, how does it feel to be last?'"

"So I said to him, 'You really want to know?' Then I dropped out of the race."

Moral of the story: Don't look down on those behind you; you might find yourself in their position someday.

MORE DAD'S COLLEGE ADVICE

Two students are renting a house in Fargo.

One winter morning while listening to the radio, they hear the announcer say, "We are going to have 3 to 4 inches of snow today. You must park your car on the even numbered side of the street, so the snowplow can get through."

So the first student goes out and moves her car.

A week later while they are eating breakfast, the radio announcer says, "We are expecting 4 to 5 inches of snow today. You must park your car on the odd numbered side of the street, so the snowplow can get through."

So the first student goes out and moves her car again.

The next week they are having breakfast again, when the radio announcer says "We are expecting 10 to 12 inches of snow today. You must park....," then the electricity goes out.

The first student says, "Oh no, I don't know what to do about the car!"

Her roommate says, "Why don't you just leave it in the garage this time?"

Moral of the story: Don't take everything literally; sometimes following the spirit of the law is more important than following the letter of the law.

MORE DAD'S COLLEGE ADVICE

A frog is born mute so he can't make any noises that a frog typically makes because, well, he can't make any noises at all. So naturally it's very difficult for the frog to make friends with the other frogs and he ends up with just one friend, a tortoise who's had the patience and the wherewithal to befriend this mute frog and to develop a system of communication with him.

Basically the frog blinks once for Yes, twice for No. The tortoise does all the talking and asks all the questions and they get along just fine. Years go by and the frog and the tortoise have fostered a beautiful friendship.

But as the frog has gotten older he has become curious about girl frogs, and desires to mingle with the other frogs his age. The tortoise senses this one day and asks the frog, "Do you want me to take you to the pond?" The frog blinks once for yes. So the tortoise takes the frog to the pond and starts introducing him to all the other frogs.

At first the frog is very nervous, but the tortoise does a great job of explaining his disability and all the other frogs are very accepting of his condition. The mute frog ends up making a lot of new friends which boosts his confidence. And then the frog spies across the pond a beautiful girl frog. He can't take his eyes off of her and the tortoise catches him staring.

The tortoise says, "You like her, don't you?"

The frog blinks once.

The tortoise says, "You want me to go talk to her for you?"

The frog blinks twice for no.

"I see," says the tortoise. "You wish you could talk to her yourself?"

The frog blinks once, a single tear rolling down his little frog cheek.

"Well gee, my friend," says the tortoise, "we've been good friends for so long, I think I owe it to you to find a way to restore your voice."

And with that the tortoise sets out. The tortoise searches all over the forest for days until one day he meets a snake who just so happened to be the most renowned surgeon of all the land. This snake could perform any surgery that exists. The tortoise explains the situation to the snake and asks him if there's anything the snake can do for the frog.

"Yessssss," the snake replies. "There issss one sssurgery I can perform that may ressstore your friend'sss voice. But you have to undersssstand, it's very risssky. There'sss a fifty percent chance your friend won't sssurvive the sssurgery."

"Oh my," says the tortoise, "I'll be sure to let him know!" So the tortoise returns to the frog and tells him the news.

"There's this snake who might be able to restore your voice, but it's a coin toss whether or not you survive the procedure. Do you want to go through with this?"

After a long pause, the frog blinks once for Yes.

So a day is set aside for the surgery and on that day all of the creatures of the forest gather around the snake and the frog as the snake prepares his tools and the anesthesia starts to kick in.

All the creatures of the forest look on anxiously, knowing that in just a few short moments they're either going to hear their friend's voice for the first time, or they're going to lose him forever.

And you'll never guess what happened next. He croaked!

Moral of the story: Being optimistic instead of pessimistic is all in how you decide to look at things.

MORE DAD'S COLLEGE ADVICE

Campus traffic officer: "I'm sorry to say this son, but it looks like your girlfriend has been hit by a truck."

Student: "Yeah... But she's got a great personality!"

Moral of the story: While you should never judge someone solely by their appearance, you should always try to make a good first impression with your own appearance.

MORE DAD'S COLLEGE ADVICE

Two students were at their work grant jobs.

The first student tells the second that she doesn't feel like being there today, so she jumps up and grabs the hanging ceiling light.

About that time their boss walks into the room and asks the first student what the hell she is doing.

The student responds: "I'm a light bulb!" The boss just shakes his head, tells her she needs some time off, and tells her to go home for the day.

As soon as the first student leaves, the second student also makes her way to the door. The boss stops the second student and asks where the hell she's going.

The second student replies, "Well, I can't work in the dark!"

Moral of the story: Work hard when required, but also make sure to carve out time for rest and relaxation; a good life requires balance.

MORE DAD'S COLLEGE ADVICE

Two college students were having a late night gab session.

The first one said to his friend, "Before I die I'm going to eat a whole bag of un-popped popcorn. Hopefully that will make the cremation a bit more interesting."

Moral of the story: Always leave 'em laughing.

MORE DAD'S COLLEGE ADVICE

Two college students were complaining about having had nothing to do on the previous weekend.

The first said, "I was so bored that I memorized six pages of a dictionary. I learned next to nothing."

Moral of the story: Instead of complaining about not having anything to do, take advantage of idle time to do something productive, like teaching yourself something new.

MORE DAD'S COLLEGE ADVICE

When Little Red Riding Hood was a college student, she was told to keep a look out for the big bad wolf.

So she's really vigilant; she walks through the forest and she spots an eye through the bush and she says, "I see you Mister Wolf!"

And the wolf runs away.

She goes deeper in the forest and she spots the wolf's ears, "I see you Mister Wolf!"

The wolf runs away again.

Little Red Riding Hood goes deeper in the forest and spots a wolf foot, "I see you Mister Wolf!"

All of a sudden the wolf screams back, "Dang you Little Red Riding Hood! Go away! I'm trying to take a dump!"

Moral of the story: Everyone needs some "me" time every now and then; make sure to take yours, and allow others to have theirs.

MORE DAD'S COLLEGE ADVICE

Two college students were talking about their families one day.

The first said, "In his spare time my dad races pigeons. But I don't know why . . . because he never wins."

Moral of the story: Don't get too hung up on whether or not you win; just do your best and enjoy the journey.

MORE DAD'S COLLEGE ADVICE

Two college students, a woman and a man, are involved in a terrible car accident. Both of their cars are totally demolished but amazingly neither of them is hurt.

After they crawl out of their cars, the woman says, "Wow, just look at our cars! There's nothing left, but fortunately we are unhurt. This must be a sign from God that we should meet and be friends and live together in peace for the rest of our days."

The man replies, "I agree with you completely. This must be a sign from God!"

The woman continues, "And look at this, here's another miracle. My car is completely demolished but this bottle of wine didn't break. Surely God wants us to drink this wine and celebrate our good fortune."

Then she hands the bottle to the man. The man nods his head in agreement, opens it, drinks half the bottle, and extends it back to the woman. But the woman politely refuses to accept the bottle.

The man asks, "Aren't you going to have any?"

The woman replies, "No, I think I'll just wait for the police...."

Moral of the story: Don't drink and drive; don't ride with someone who has been drinking; and don't drink with someone waiting for the police.

MORE DAD'S COLLEGE ADVICE

The blonde college student came home from her first day commuting into the city for her internship.

Her roommate noticed she was looking a little peaked and asked, "Are you feeling all right?"

"Not really," she replied.

"I'm nauseous from sitting backward on the train."

"Poor dear," the roommate said. "Why didn't you ask the person sitting across from you to switch seats for a while?"

"I couldn't," she replied. "There was no one there."

Moral of the story: Choose to look forward to where you're going, instead of lamenting where you've come from.

MORE DAD'S COLLEGE ADVICE

Two blonde students are putting siding on a house; one is on the ground cutting the pieces and handing them up to the other who nails them in.

The blonde on the ladder throws every second or third nail away, which then fall and hit the blonde on the ground on the head.

The blond on the ground asks the top blonde, "Why are you throwing those nails away?"

She explains that the tossed nails are defective.

"What do you mean they are defective?"

The blonde explains that when she takes a nail out of the pouch, if it is pointed towards the house she pounds it in, but if it points away from the house it must be defective.

The blonde on the ground shouts, "You idiot! They're not defective. They're for the other side of the house!"

Moral of the story: Be gracious and humble when working with others; just because they are wrong, it doesn't necessarily mean that you are right.

MORE DAD'S COLLEGE ADVICE

Two students were having a late night session of solving the world's problems and other general philosophical musings, when the first one had a bit of a "eureka moment."

"I just realized something. I know why dinosaurs can't clap," he said excitedly to his friend.

"Well, tell me. I wanna know too. Why can't dinosaurs clap?"

"Because they're dead."

Moral of the story: People learn at different speeds, and it's not really a race, so enjoy your "eureka moments"; and help others enjoy their own "eureka moments".

MORE DAD'S COLLEGE ADVICE

A not so bright college student had always wanted to travel abroad. She had saved her money for several years, and finally had enough for her dream vacation.

Until now, she'd never even been out of the country, so naturally she needed a passport. She went to the Passport Office and asked what she needed to do in order to get a passport.

"You must take the loyalty oath first," responded the passport clerk. "Raise your right hand, please."

The student raised her right hand. "Do you swear to defend the Constitution of the United States against all its enemies, foreign or domestic?"

The student's face turned pale and her voice trembled as she asked in a small voice, "Ummm . . . . all by myself?"

Moral of the story: It's okay to ask for help when things get tough; no one is on this earth alone.

MORE DAD'S COLLEGE ADVICE

Two college students are stranded in the desert, dying of thirst. As they walk, with all hope lost, one of them spots a well in the middle of the desert.

"Look! A well!" said the first student.

"There is no way that well has water," replied the second.

"Maybe we should check if it has water. Look, let's drop that rock into the well to check whether it has or not," offered the first student optimistically.

It took both students working together to carry the big rock. It was a huge effort, but it was the only rock in sight.

They dropped it into the well, and then heard a huge splash.

"See? I knew it would have water. We're saved!' said the first student. And then surprisingly, as he spoke, a goat suddenly jumped into the well. "Look! Even the animals get their water from here, let's get some too!"

As they were about to descend into the well, a shepherd passed by in his car and stopped near the two stranded students.

"Have you guys by chance seen my goat?" asked the shepherd.

"Yeah. We just saw it jump into this well right here!"

"That's impossible," replied the shepherd, "I tied it up to a huge rock so it wouldn't run away!"

Moral of the story: Check if there are any strings attached before entering into a joint venture, especially if things look too good to be true.

MORE DAD'S COLLEGE ADVICE

A college student was complaining to his roommate about one of his classes.

"I passed all my courses except for Greek mythology. The whole semester it's been my Achilles' elbow."

Moral of the story: Don't expect perfection in every subject; there's always one that will be "Greek" to you.

MORE DAD'S COLLEGE ADVICE

A college student was visiting her grandparents.

Her grandfather said to her, "Go get me a newspaper."

The student laughed at him and said, "Oh grandpa . . . . you're so old. Just use my phone."

So he took her phone and slammed it against the wall to kill a spider.

Moral of the story: Respect your elders; they're smarter and more with it than you think they are.

MORE DAD'S COLLEGE ADVICE

Two college students were talking over lunch one day.

The first one said, "I bought a toilet brush since I had noticed seeing one in pretty much everyone else's bathroom. But after giving it a try for a week I decided to go back to using toilet paper."

Moral of the story: Don't assume you know how to do something new; don't be afraid to ask for help if you don't know how to do something.

MORE DAD'S COLLEGE ADVICE

Two college students were sharing stories about growing up.

The first one said, "I remember one summer day, I was swimming at the local pool and had nature call. So I decided to have a sneaky pee in the deep end. But I think the lifeguard must have noticed, because he blew his whistle so stinkin' loud that I almost fell in."

Moral of the story: Go places you never dreamed you'd be able to go; just don't go places where no one is supposed to go.

MORE DAD'S COLLEGE ADVICE

A college student asked her roommate how her new shoes were working out.

The roommate replied, "I didn't think wearing orthopedic shoes would help . . . . but now, I stand corrected."

Moral of the story: Proper footwear makes all the difference in the world . . . . especially when sole searching.

MORE DAD'S COLLEGE ADVICE

A group of college students were chastising one of their study group members for continually telling bad jokes.

"Don't interrupt our study group if you're only going to tell 'dad' jokes," one complained.

"Well, how am I supposed to know if a joke is a 'dad' joke?" he asked.

"It'll be apparent because it's full groan."

Moral of the story: Humor is a dangerous weapon; use it only for good, never for evil; meaning, don't make fun of people, because that's just not nice.

MORE DAD'S COLLEGE ADVICE

A blonde college student is driving down the highway, when she sees another blonde student in a field trying to row a canoe across the grass.

The first blonde student, infuriated, stops her car, gets out, and starts shouting at the other blonde student.

"People like you are why everyone thinks blondes are dumb!! I swear to God, if I could swim I'd go out there and kick your butt!"

Moral of the story: Don't assume that you're immune from making mistakes just because you recognize a mistake that someone else is making; everyone makes mistakes; they're for learning from, not for berating people over.

MORE DAD'S COLLEGE ADVICE

Two college students were talking one day.

The first one said, "I generally consider myself a modest and humble person. Basically it's what makes me so amazingly awesome."

Moral of the story: Always be humble and thankful for the gifts that God has given you.

MORE DAD'S COLLEGE ADVICE

A photon checks into a hotel.

The college student bellhop asks, "Can I help you with your luggage?"

The photon replies, "I don't have any. I'm traveling light."

Moral of the story: Pack appropriately when traveling; it makes any trip much more enjoyable.

MORE DAD'S COLLEGE ADVICE

One day a college student walked into a classroom with a newt on his shoulder.

Seeing this, the professor said, "What an interesting pet. What's its name?"

"Tiny," the student replies.

"What an odd name; why do you call him Tiny?"

"Because...it's my newt."

Moral of the story: Always take time to laugh and enjoy life even if it's just a short joke that can be told in less than a minute.

MORE DAD'S COLLEGE ADVICE

A college student landed an internship with a personal security firm. He was very excited to learn that he'd be working as a body guard for Don Smith, the wealthy CEO of a large corporation.

One day as the CEO was walking out of a large trade show and heading toward his limo, a possible assassin stepped forward and aimed a gun towards the CEO.

The college student intern reacted by jumping up and shouting, "Mickey Mouse!"

This startled the 'would be' assassin and he was immediately captured.

Later, the intern's supervisor took him aside and asked him, "Now, what in the world made you shout 'Mickey Mouse'?"

Blushing, the college intern replied, "I got nervous. I meant to shout...... 'Donald, duck'."

Moral of the story: It's okay to be nervous in new situations; just do your best and let the chips fall where they may. You may even end up being happily surprised with the results.

MORE DAD'S COLLEGE ADVICE

One day a college student came back to his room to find that his roommate had just bought a couple of goldfish.

So he asked his roommate, "What are you going to name them?"

His roommate replied, "The name of the first is 'One', and the other's name is 'Two'."

"Why on earth would you give your goldfish names like that?" he asked his roommate.

"Well," came the answer, "if 'One' dies I'll still have 'Two'."

Moral of the story: Always keep a positive attitude, especially when things aren't going the way you'd hoped they would.

MORE DAD'S COLLEGE ADVICE

A college student walks into a bar and says to the bartender, "If I show you a really good trick, will you give me a free drink?"

The bartender considers and then agrees to the proposition.

The student reaches into his pocket and pulls out a tiny mouse. He reaches into his other pocket and pulls out a tiny piano. The mouse stretches, cracks his knuckles, and proceeds to play the blues.

The bartender is amazed, and pours the student a drink on the house as the student puts the mouse and piano away.

After the student finishes his drink, he asks the bartender, "If I show you an even better trick, will you give me free drinks for the rest of the evening?"

The bartender agrees, thinking that no trick could possibly be better than the first.

The student reaches into his pockets again and pulls out the tiny mouse and tiny piano. The mouse stretches, cracks his knuckles, and proceeds to play the blues. The student reaches into a third pocket and pulls out a small bullfrog, who begins to sing along with the mouse's music.

Again the bartender is amazed.

While the student is enjoying his free beverages, a stranger approaches him and offers him $100,000 for the bullfrog.

"Sorry," the student replies, "he's not for sale."

The stranger increases the offer to $250,000, cash up front.

"No," the student insists, "he's not for sale."

The stranger again increases the offer, this time to $500,000 cash.

The student finally agrees, and turns the frog over to the stranger in exchange for the money.

"Are you insane?" the bartender exclaimed. "That frog could have been worth millions to you, and you let him go for a mere $500,000!"

"Don't worry about it," the student answered. "The frog was nothing special. You see, the mouse is a ventriloquist."

Moral of the story: Things aren't always what they seem; make sure you research before making a large expenditure.

MORE DAD'S COLLEGE ADVICE

A boy asked his mother one day, "Mom? What's dark humor?"

"Well son...you see that college student, with no arms, sitting over there? Tell him to clap."

"Mom! You know I'm blind."

"Exactly."

Moral of the story: Don't take advantage of folks with disabilities, but don't be patronizing to them either.

MORE DAD'S COLLEGE ADVICE

A college student was complaining, to his roommate about how he didn't understand his girlfriend.

"The other day she yelled at me, 'Are you even listening to me?' and I thought 'What a strange way to start a conversation.'"

Moral of the story: If you want people to give you their full attention, then make sure that you give them your full attention.

MORE DAD'S COLLEGE ADVICE

There once was a college student named Bob. He had a lifelong friend since grade school named Derwerld.

They always got along great and had a running joke where Bob would tease Derwerld about his unusual name, and Derwerld would tease Bob about his plain ordinary name.

One day, Bob found out that his girlfriend was cheating on him, with none other than his best friend Derwerld!

Distraught and angry over the matter, Bob, vented to some of his fellow college students.

A majority of the group convinced Bob to exact revenge on Derwerld by blackmailing him. Bob figured that this would be easy to do because Derwerld was constantly cheating on his exams.

Bob also had a friend named Bahdi who was a bit of a psychic. Bahdi warned Bob that he should steer clear of Derwerld, otherwise Derwerld would be the death of him. But Bob dismissed the warning as nonsense.

But Bob's desire for revenge was too strong, so he decided to blackmail Derwerld.

One day, Bob sat behind Derwerld in a lecture hall and took a video of him obviously cheating on an exam.

He then sent Derwerld an email, in which he threatened to send the video to Derwerld's professor and the college dean, unless Derwerld paid Bob $5,000.

Derwerld responded via email asking Bob to meet him at the Kagadil Farm at high noon the next day.

Bob agreed, but as a precaution took another friend named Sam with him, as he was nervous about the meeting.

When they arrived at the farm, Bob and Sam were surprised to see Derwerld, sitting on top of a steamroller. And before they realized what was happening, Derwerld had started the steamroller moving and ran over Bob with it.

Bob, his body broken, battered and bruised, spoke these final words to his friend:

"Sam, Bahdi once told me Derwerld was gonna roll me."

Moral of the story: It's best to just move on from a bad situation. Retaliation and revenge usually end up hurting you just as much, and sometimes more, than it does the intended target.

MORE DAD'S COLLEGE ADVICE

A blonde college student gets on a plane to Detroit and heads for a seat in first class, even though she only purchased an economy ticket. A short while into the flight an air hostess notices that the blonde college student is sitting in the wrong section of the plane and asks her to return to her allocated seat. The blonde simply replies "no".

Shocked and confused, the hostess insists once more that she move, but the blond refuses again. The hostess leaves to go get help from other attendants. Multiple attendants try their luck at explaining to the blond that she's in the wrong seat, but none prevail. Eventually, they seek the help of the Captain.

"She's blonde, you say?" queries the Captain. The attendants all nod. "I know how to handle this," he says, "my wife is a blonde too."

The Captain gets up and approaches the blonde student while the flight attendants watch from a distance. After a few seconds the blond student quickly gathers her things and heads back to her seat in the economy section of the plane.

The Captain returns to the attendants. Amazed, they ask how he did it.

"It's simple, really," he said, "I just told her that first class wasn't flying to Detroit."

Moral of the story: There are more ways than just one to reach your destination. Don't get distraught when life throws up detours, just think of it as taking the scenic route.

MORE DAD'S COLLEGE ADVICE

A college student fighter pilot and a college student cargo pilot are both out flying around, talking smack to each other on the radio.

The fighter pilot goes on about how much cooler he is than the cargo pilot and says, "Watch this, bro!" Then he hits the afterburners, does a barrel roll, and then a loop. "Top that!" he shouts to the cargo pilot.

"Ok, well watch this," says the cargo pilot. The fighter pilot watches as the cargo plane just goes straight for a while.

"How'd you like that?" asks the cargo pilot.

The fighter pilot is confused and asks, "What did you do?"

The cargo pilot replies, "I used the bathroom, then went to the galley and got myself some more coffee. Let's see you do that!"

Moral of the story: Fancy may look fun, but often it's not very practical; pick substance over style, for the long run.

MORE DAD'S COLLEGE ADVICE

A college student is late for an exam. But he can't find a place to park. In desperation, he begins to pray.

"Please Lord, if you help me find a parking spot right now, I promise to go to church every Sunday and never put off studying again!"

A moment later, he sees a beautiful empty spot right next to the entrance.

"Never mind. Found one!"

Moral of the story: Look for God in small things and give thanks, even if it's just for finding a pen to take notes with, or finding a place to park.

MORE DAD'S COLLEGE ADVICE

A college student with authority walked into a bar.

And ordered everyone a round.

Moral of the story: Don't be bossy; people don't always like being told that they have to do something. Try giving suggestions instead.

MORE DAD'S COLLEGE ADVICE

There once was a college student who spent a summer working as a safari guide in Africa, and one day he was leading a tour through the grasslands when he encountered an elephant standing on three legs. He watched this elephant for a minute and it didn't move, so he decided to investigate.

Leaving his tour group behind, he approached the animal slowly, so as to not disturb him. When he got close enough he saw a small thorny branch stuck in the elephant's front right foot, and ever so carefully he pulled it out.

The elephant let out a whimper as it put its foot down, realizing it could walk again without pain. The elephant stood staring straight at the guide for a while, before the animal went on its way, and the tour guide on his.

Several months later the college student tour guide was going through the San Diego Zoo while on vacation; as he passed the elephant enclosure he noticed an elephant looking at him. "You look familiar...," he said. The elephant didn't reply, for he could not speak, but it stared back.

After a moment of staring, the elephant raised his front right foot. "It's you!!" the student exclaimed. And he hopped into the enclosure without a second thought. He ran up to the elephant with joy in his heart, ready for a loving embrace!

And in a single smooth motion the elephant picked him up with its trunk and slammed him on the ground, killing him instantly. It was not the same elephant.

Moral of the story: Don't assume people will act the way you want them to; they may be having a bad day.

MORE DAD'S COLLEGE ADVICE

An American college student was talking with his Irish roommate named Paddy.

"Paddy, why is it that whenever you ask an Irishman a question, he answers with another question?"

"Who told you that?" asked Paddy.

Moral of the story: Don't be afraid to ask follow up questions if you don't understand the initial answer; and don't forget to take your allergy medicine.

MORE DAD'S COLLEGE ADVICE

Two college roommates were talking about what they'd learned in their respective history classes.

The first one said, "Here are some interesting Gandhi facts."

"Mahatma Gandhi walked barefoot everywhere, to the extent that his feet became quite thick and hard."

"He was also a spiritual person. Even when on hunger strike, he did not eat much and became thin and frail."

"Furthermore, due to his diet of raw grains, he ended up with very bad breath."

"Therefore he came to be known as a 'super calloused fragile mystic plagued with halitosis'."

Moral of the story: Wear proper shoes; say your prayers; eat a balanced diet; and use your SmartMouth™ Original Activated Mouthwash every day.

MORE DAD'S COLLEGE ADVICE

There was once a college student named Gérard Leahey, who gave up his college career to be a "Bingo Caller." He started this career innocently enough, when in high school his teacher asked him to call the numbers in a bingo based game that is supposed to help kids with math. The teacher, who would usually call the numbers, had a sore throat. Gérard found that he could be charmingly entertaining while calling, without disrupting the flow of the game.

After high school, he enrolled in college as an art history major. While attending college, he chanced to be asked to help out at a charity fund raiser. The fund raiser, you guessed it, was a bingo and he provided the service of caller. He easily found his pace, and it was generally agreed he was the best caller the regulars had ever heard.

One player suggested he work weekends at the usual bingo hall she frequented. It turns out that good Bingo Callers are a highly sought after commodity, and fair sized bingo halls pay a good buck for "talent." That and they also get paid tips.

Gérard had stumbled into a job that he thought at first would be merely jingle change. But on these weekends he would develop his timing, his patter, his clever tagline commentary "clickety-click, sixty-six" and the like. The bingo hall proprietor soon asked him to work full time. And so his art history classes became history.

After several long years Gérard became somewhat of a celebrity - at least in the small town in which he worked. He had stopped working weekends long ago in favor of the weekdays and some evenings which featured younger, more interactive crowds. Gérard was happy.

So it is not without a bit of irony that what lead to Gérard's later difficulties occurred at a charity function at the very venue where his career was launched. It was, however, a function for seniors. While Gérard felt obliged to help out, he did not look forward to it. And sure enough, his trademark quick style and banter were met with shouts of, "Slow down, sonny!" and "Could you repeat that!"

211

It put him off his game causing him to become restless and bored. Between each number call he had to wait, and wait, and wait, while watching a sea of bobbing blue haired heads wave through the room amid the soft "mooud, mooud" sound of bingo dabbers. To keep his sanity between numbers he would fidget. He called one number, then grabbed the next (as was his custom) and while waiting to call the number in his hand he would toss the ball into the air and catch it in his shirt pocket... catch it behind his back... catch it in his teeth.

It was with this last stunt that it happened. Just as he caught the ball in his teeth, a little old lady in the table just in front of him yelled, "BINGO!" with a force that startled him. He "Ulped!", and swallowed the ball he had just deftly caught. With all the attention on the winner, no one had noticed. And Gérard was not about to let such an incident affect his reputation, so he told no one. He confirmed the winner, finished his duties for the evening, collected his pay then quietly left.

But later that evening it started. The nausea. The bloated feeling in his gut. The discomfort while going to the bathroom. It was too much. The next day he was a wreck.

So he went to the emergency room. Not trusting doctor/patient confidentiality, Gérard described his symptoms but did not explain the incident. He was too embarrassed to go into detail about swallowing a bingo ball.

The puzzled doctor took X-Rays. After examining them he said to Gérard, "You have the strangest tumor I've ever seen. But don't worry. It's benign."

Moral of the story: Be upfront and honest when asking people for help, otherwise they won't be able to properly assist you.

MORE DAD'S COLLEGE ADVICE

Two college students were talking about things they liked to do outside of class.

The first one said, "I like to play chess with old men in the park. Although it is hard to find thirty-two of them."

Moral of the story: Always make an effort to include others in your activities.

MORE DAD'S COLLEGE ADVICE

Two college students were talking about their families one day.

The first one said, "My dad has a pencil that was once owned by Shakespeare. He once went to have it appraised, but it's so chewed up that they couldn't tell if it was 2B or not 2B."

Moral of the story: Chew gum not pencils; and if you don't know what a 2B pencil is, then this advice is much a chew about nothing.

MORE DAD'S COLLEGE ADVICE

A college student is working as a waiter in a restaurant. He is called over by a man to whom he had just given a bowl of soup.

The man says to the student, "Waiter, come taste the soup."

Waiter says, "Is something wrong with the soup?"

Guy says, "Taste the soup."

Waiter says, "Is there something wrong with the soup? Is the soup too hot?"

Guy says, "Will you taste the soup?"

"What's wrong, is the soup too cold?"

"Will you just taste the soup?!"

"All right already! I'll taste the soup - where's the spoon??"

"Aha! There is no spoon!"

Moral of the story: If you have a beef with someone, be upfront with them and just tell them what is bothering you. Do it in a polite way, but also in a direct way that doesn't make them guess what the issue is.

MORE DAD'S COLLEGE ADVICE

A German college student told his roommate about his eight-year old brother who had never spoken a word.

One afternoon, as his brother sat eating his lunch he turned to his mother and said, "The soup is cold."

His astonished mother exclaimed, "Son, I've waited so long to hear you speak. But all these years you never said a thing. Why haven't you spoken before?"

The boy looked at her and replied, "Up until now, everything has been satisfactory."

Moral of the story: Don't be a chronic complainer; make sure to tell people thank you, even if things are "just" satisfactory. Giving people compliments is the best way to build them up.

MORE DAD'S COLLEGE ADVICE

A Polish college student went to the DMV to apply for a driver's license. First, of course, he had to take an eyesight test. The optician showed him a card with the letters 'C Z W I N O S T A C Z.'

"Can you read this?" the optician asked.

"Read it?" the Polish student replied, "I went to grade school with the guy."

Moral of the story: Broaden your horizons; get to know people who don't come from the same background as you.

MORE DAD'S COLLEGE ADVICE

Two college students were talking over coffee.

The first one asked, "What's the difference between in-laws and outlaws?"

His friend answered, "Outlaws are wanted."

Moral of the story: Be accepting of new family members (and friends), just like my father-in-law who always said that in-laws should be called outlaws.

MORE DAD'S COLLEGE ADVICE

Two college law students took a break from studying.

The first one said to his friend, "When I become a lawyer, I want to defend a penguin."

"Why do you want to defend a penguin?"

"Just so I can say the words 'Your Honor, clearly my client is not a flight risk.'"

Moral of the story: Be nice to lawyers; some of them are people too.

MORE DAD'S COLLEGE ADVICE

A college student, stressing over finals, is outside of a candy shop, shoveling candy in his mouth.

A man approaches the student and says, "Don't eat candy, kid. It's not good for you."

The student replies, "My grandfather lived until he was 97."

"Really," says the man. "Did he eat a lot of candy, too?"

The student replies, "No. But he minded his own stinkin' business!"

Moral of the story: Unless a person asks you to get involved, it's best to mind your own stinkin' business. And don't mess with people who are stressing over finals.

MORE DAD'S COLLEGE ADVICE

A college student comes up to the US border on a bicycle. He's got two large bags over his shoulders. The guard stops him and says, "What's in the bags?"

"Sand," answered the student.

The guard says, "We'll just see about that. Get off the bike." After the student gets off the bike, the guard takes the bags and rips them apart; he empties them out and finds nothing in them but sand. He detains the student overnight and has the sand analyzed, only to discover that there is nothing but pure sand in the bags. The guard releases the student, puts the sand into new bags, hefts them onto the student's shoulders, and lets him pedal his bike across the border.

A week later, the same thing happens. The guard asks, "What have you got?"

"Sand," says student.

The guard makes the student get off the bike again, does his thorough examination and again discovers that the bags contain nothing but sand. He gives the sand back to the student, and the student crosses the border on the bicycle. This sequence of events is repeated every day for three years.

Finally, the student doesn't show up one day and the guard runs into him, by coincidence, in a local college bar. "Hey buddy," says the guard, "I know you are smuggling something. It's driving me crazy. It's all I think about, and I can't sleep. Just between you and me, what are you smuggling?"

The college student sips his beer, smiles, and says, "Bicycles."

Moral of the story: Sometimes what you need is right under your nose, being ignored, while you mistakenly look for things you want, but don't really need.

MORE DAD'S COLLEGE ADVICE

A group of college students were hanging out one day when one of them said, "Here's something you may not know about me. I can cut wood just by looking at it."

"No way," came the reply.

"It's true. I saw it with my own eyes."

Moral of the story: Don't believe everything you see and hear; there is more than one side to every story.

MORE DAD'S COLLEGE ADVICE

A college student had two pet birds. They were both parrots.

One day both parrots were sitting on a perch when one turned to the other and said, "Something smells fishy."

Moral of the story: If you don't like the view from where you're standing, don't just whine and complain about it, work to make a positive change in your situation.

MORE DAD'S COLLEGE ADVICE

Two college students were talking about their respective spring breaks.

The first one said, "One morning I saw a neighbor talking to her cat. It was obvious that the crazy lady thought her cat could understand her. So I went home and told my dog about it. We laughed a lot."

Moral of the story: Don't be too quick to dismiss others as eccentric, or others might be inclined to judge you in the same manner.

MORE DAD'S COLLEGE ADVICE

Two college students were talking about what they did on their respective spring breaks.

The first one said, "I went by the house I grew up in. I went up to the door and asked if I could go in and look around. They said 'No!' and slammed the door in my face. ... My parents can be such jerks."

Moral of the story: Be nice to your parents and to other people in general, if you want them to be nice to you.

MORE DAD'S COLLEGE ADVICE

Three college students went to a country park and were laying in the grass under a tree near a country road.

Nothing happens for a while, but then a car passes by.

After half an hour, the first student says: "BMW."

Another hour passes and the second student says: "Mercedes."

Another two hours pass and the third student stands up to leave, and before going away says: "I can't stand hanging around with the two of you. You're arguing all the time."

Moral of the story: Don't insist on always being 'right'; sometimes it's better to lose an argument and keep a friend, than it is to win an argument but lose a friend.

MORE DAD'S COLLEGE ADVICE

A college student was taking a paleontology class to satisfy his earth sciences requirement.

He looked at the last question on his final exam, "Explain why dinosaurs became extinct."

For his answer he wrote the following:

Three carnivorous dinosaurs found a magic lamp with a genie inside. The genie says "I can give you all one wish. Anything your heart desires!"

The first dinosaur says, "I want a big piece of juicy meat!" And he is given the biggest piece of meat any of them had ever seen.

The second dinosaur, in an attempt to 'one up' the first, says, "I want a big meat shower!" And he is showered in delicious meat.

The third dinosaur, not to be outdone by the other two, says "I want a big meatier shower!"

Moral of the story: Don't be greedy for material things; it's better to appreciate what you have than to be jealous of what others have.

MORE DAD'S COLLEGE ADVICE

A college student was studying in her dorm room when she heard her roommate come back from class.

"How was your English test today?" she asked.

"It was easy except I had trouble on this one difficult question," her roommate said.

"What was the question?" the student replied.

"It asked for the past tense of think."

"What did you put for your answer?"

"I couldn't really figure it out. I thought and thought and thought and thought, but I finally just gave up and wrote 'thunk'."

Moral of the story: Some say English is difficult; it can be understood through tough thorough thought, though... so study hard.

MORE DAD'S COLLEGE ADVICE

Two college students were talking about how difficult it is to make changes in their lives.

The first one said, "I decided to cut ties with all the people weighing me down. ... But my climbing partner didn't appreciate it."

Moral of the story: Choose your friends wisely; they can hold you down, or they can help you soar.

MORE DAD'S COLLEGE ADVICE

A college student walks into a commons area with his phone in hand. He suddenly realizes he needs to fart. Thinking quickly, he logs into his music streaming service and turns up the volume, thinking that if the music is loud enough, then no one will hear his flatulence.

After he's got the volume at maximum level, he farts. But when looking around he sees that everyone has turned their heads and are now starting at him.

That's when he remembers that he was listening to his music with earbuds.

Moral of the story: Pay attention to your surroundings by taking your earbuds out, and go use the bathroom if you gotta do that sort of thing.

MORE DAD'S COLLEGE ADVICE

Two blonde students were driving down the road, at the start of a road trip.

The blonde student driving asked her friend in the passenger seat to look and see if the turn signal was working.

So the other blonde student looked out the window and answered, "Yes....No....Yes....No...."

Moral of the story: Always make sure your vehicle is in good working order before leaving on a trip, and always remember to use your turn signals.

MORE DAD'S COLLEGE ADVICE

A college student was talking to his roommate.

"I gave up my seat to a blind person on the bus. . . . That's how I lost my job as a bus driver."

Moral of the story: It's good to be nice to others, but not to the point that it costs you your livelihood.

MORE DAD'S COLLEGE ADVICE

One day while a blonde college student was out driving her car, she bumped into the back of a truck.

The truck driver was so angry that he made her pull over into a parking lot and then get out of her car. Then he took a piece of chalk and drew a circle on the pavement. He ordered her to stand in the middle of the circle and that not under any circumstance was she to even think about leaving the circle.

Still furious, he went over to her car and slashed the tires. The blonde started laughing.

This made the man angrier so he smashed her windshield. And the blonde laughed even harder.

Livid, the man broke all the remaining windows and keyed her car.

The blonde is now laughing hysterically, so the truck driver asks her what's so funny.

The blonde giggled and replied, "When you weren't looking, I stepped out of the circle three times!"

Moral of the story: Sometimes it's good fun to be a rebel, but be a smart rebel.

MORE DAD'S COLLEGE ADVICE

A college student was puzzling over his homework when he decided to ask his roommate for help.

"Hey, can you give me examples of jobs that aren't around anymore?"

"Steve," he answered.

Moral of the story: Remember that all your learning comes on the shoulders of those who have gone before you; be humbly grateful for the legacy they have left you.

MORE DAD'S COLLEGE ADVICE

Two college students who happened to be avid outdoorsmen were chatting over a late night snack.

"What's the most exciting outdoor adventure you've had?" asked the first.

"Probably the time I caught a bear," said the second.

"Dude, that's crazy! You actually caught a real live bear?"

"Yes, I did."

"I'd love to do that someday. So tell me, how do you catch a bear?"

"Well, first you have to dig a deep hole in the woods and fill it half-full of ashes from the fireplace. Then place peas all around the outside of the hole, because believe it or not, bears absolutely love peas. And finally, you hide in some nearby bushes and wait for a bear to come by."

"And then what?"

"And then when a bear comes by to take a pea, you kick him in the ash hole."

Moral of the story: Be nice to everyone, even if they seem to resemble an ash hole, and make that sure people can differentiate between you and an ash hole.

MORE DAD'S COLLEGE ADVICE

Two college students were talking about their pets back home.

"We have a magic dog," said the first.

"Really?" replied his friend incredulously. "A magic dog?"

"Yep. It's a Labracadabrador. We call him Hairy Houndini."

Moral of the story: It's good to be kind to animals, but it's more important to be kind to people.

MORE DAD'S COLLEGE ADVICE

A blond college student is driving a helicopter and it crashes.

When the police come and ask the blond college student what happened she says, "I got cold, so I turned off the big fan!"

Moral of the story: Don't insist on changing things just for your own convenience; there may be a very good reason for things being done the way they are.

MORE DAD'S COLLEGE ADVICE

Two college students were talking over lunch.

The first one said, "My girlfriend's dog died, so I tried to cheer her up by getting her an identical one."

"Good idea. Did it cheer her up?" his friend asked.

"No. It just made her more upset. She screamed at me, 'What am I supposed to do with two dead dogs?'"

Moral of the story: Remember to comfort the sorrowful.

MORE DAD'S COLLEGE ADVICE

Two sisters, who were college students, one blonde and one brunette, inherit the family ranch. Unfortunately, after just a few years, they are in financial trouble. In order to keep the bank from repossessing the ranch, they need to purchase a bull so that they can breed their own stock. The brunette balances their checkbook, then takes their last $600 dollars out west to another ranch where a man has a prize bull for sale.

Upon leaving, she tells her sister, "When I get there, if I decide to buy the bull, I'll contact you to drive out after me and haul it home." The brunette arrives at the man's ranch, inspects the bull, and decides she does want to buy it. The man tells her that he can sell it for $599, no less. After paying him, she drives to the nearest town to send her sister a telegram to tell her the news.

She walks into the telegraph office, and says, "I want to send a telegram to my sister telling her that I've bought a bull for our ranch. I need her to hitch the trailer to our pick-up truck and drive out here so we can haul it home."

The telegraph operator explains that he'll be glad to help her, then adds, "It's just 99 cents a word."

Well, with only $1 left after paying for the bull, the brunette realizes that she'll only be able to send her sister one word. After thinking for a few minutes, she nods, and says, "I want you to send her the word, 'comfortable.'"

The telegraph operator shakes his head. "How is she ever going to know that you want her to hitch the trailer to your pick-up truck and drive out here to haul that bull back to your ranch if you send her just the one word, 'comfortable'?"

The brunette explains, "My sister's blonde. She'll read it slow."

Moral of the story: Take the time to explain things in a way that others will understand.

MORE DAD'S COLLEGE ADVICE

A college student was grocery shopping and while in the market came across a classmate who appeared to be very agitated.

"Hey man, what's wrong?" he asked.

"Well," the classmate answered, "My roommate asked me to put tomato ketchup on the shopping list that I was writing out. And now I can't read a stinkin' word on the list."

Moral of the story: Never go grocery shopping when you're hungry, and always make a list first.

MORE DAD'S COLLEGE ADVICE

Two college students were up late one night talking about life.

The first one asked, "What is the most difficult thing about yourself that you've had to deal with?"

His friend considered the question silently for a moment, and then answered, "Well . . . I used to be addicted to the Hokey Pokey. But then I turned myself around."

Moral of the story: Life is short; don't forget to make time to dance to the music.

MORE DAD'S COLLEGE ADVICE

A college student met up with a friend for lunch, just after his architecture design class.

His friend said, "You look like you're in a bad mood. Something happen in your architecture design class?"

"Well, my professor kicked me out of class."

"Kicked you out of class? Why?"

"Because he didn't like how I solved a problem."

"What was the problem?"

"He asked, 'How would you light a soccer stadium'."

"And what was your answer?"

"With a soccer match."

Moral of the story: Even when things look darkest, there is always light to be found; sometimes you have to turn around to see it, but it is there.

MORE DAD'S COLLEGE ADVICE

A college student met up with a friend for lunch, just after his medical pathology class.

His friend said, "You look like you're in a bad mood. Something happen in your medical pathology class?"

"Well, my professor kicked me out of class."

"Kicked you out of class? Why?"

"Because he didn't like how I answered a question."

"What was the question?"

"He asked, 'What's the difference between the bird flu and the swine flu?'."

"And what was your answer?"

"One requires a tweetment, and the other requires an oinkment."

Moral of the story: Make sure your solution appropriately addresses the problem; otherwise you risk exasperating the issue.

MORE DAD'S COLLEGE ADVICE

A college student was sitting at a bar one night when an Asian looking student sits down next to next to him and takes a sip of beer.

The first student glanced over at him and asked the new student if he knew any of those martial arts like Kung Fu, or Karate or Ju Jitsu.

The Asian looking student says, "No! What the heck, dude!? Are you asking because I'm Chinese?"

The first student said, "No, I'm asking because you're drinking MY beer."

Moral of the story: Don't take other peoples' stuff; and don't be starting a fight just because someone takes a sip of your drink.

MORE DAD'S COLLEGE ADVICE

A college student was coming out of Easter services at church, and the preacher was standing at the door as he always is to shake hands.

The preacher grabbed the student by the hand and pulled him aside and said to him, "You need to join the Army of the Lord!"

The student replied, "I'm already in the Army of the Lord, Pastor."

The pastor questioned, "If you're in the Army of the Lord, then how come I don't see you except at Christmas and Easter?"

The student whispered back, "I'm in the secret service."

Moral of the story: It's good to take time to build up your faith life.

MORE DAD'S COLLEGE ADVICE

Two college students were studying for finals when the first one stated, "An apple pie costs $7.95 in Jamaica."

"But In Cuba," he continued, "you will have to pay $9.90 for an apple pie."

"Whereas in Barbados you will only spend $4.50 for an apple pie."

"And these, my friend, are the Pie Rates of the Caribbean."

Moral of the story: always shop around to make sure that you are getting a good price, especially if you are purchasing a big ticket item.

MORE DAD'S COLLEGE ADVICE

Two college roommates, who happened to be man and wife, are sitting down to dinner, during summer break. "Ringling Brothers is coming to town this week," she said. "The poster says they have a dancing bear. I always wanted to see one of those."

"Maybe next year," says the man. "Work's really busy this week."

The next night at dinner, the man can barely sit down before his wife starts talking excitedly. "The neighbors went to the show today and said the tightrope walkers were doing the Hokey Pokey right up there on the wire! Can you even imagine?"

"I'd love to take you," said the man. "But the boss will be mad if I don't get this project finished."

The following night the wife gushed about how the paperboy told her about how a dozen clowns had popped out of this tiny car and then did the can-can in bloomers and that it was about the funniest thing he ever saw. The man was starting to feel a little bad that he couldn't take her, but work was work.

The next night, the wife was downcast. "My book club said last night that the lion tamer and the girl who rides the elephants did a waltz and it was just perfectly romantic," she said. "It feels like we're the only people in town who haven't seen the show yet, and they only have one more performance, tomorrow! Oh please can't we go?"

The man thinks it over and decides that this might be the only opportunity for them to see such a thing, and maybe work can wait. He calls his friend to ask him to cover for him at work the next day, and the man and his wife go to bed excited about seeing the show.

The next day at work the boss notices the man is out and asks the friend about it. "Oh," says the friend. "He can't come in today, four unseen circus dances."

Moral of the story: Work is good, but time with family is gooder.

MORE DAD'S COLLEGE ADVICE

There were three students, an Englishman, a Scotsman, and an Irishman, all doing work grant jobs on the top of a cliff.

The Englishman said, "If I have cheese in my sandwich tomorrow, I'll jump off this cliff."

The Scotsman said, "If I have jam in my sandwich tomorrow, I'll jump off the cliff."

The Irishman said, "If I have ham tomorrow, I'll jump off the cliff."

The next day, the Englishman had cheese, the Irishman had ham, and the Scotsman had jam. So they all jumped.

At the funerals, the moms of the Scotsman and Englishman said, "Why didn't they just tell us they didn't like their sandwiches?"

The Irish mom said, "I don't know why my student jumped off the cliff. He made his own sandwiches."

Moral of the story: If you don't like the way things are, instead of just complaining, work to make a positive change.

MORE DAD'S COLLEGE ADVICE

A college student received a text from his roommate.

The message said, "The man who invented auto-correct has died. His funfair is on sundial at moon. May he restaurant in piece, he will be mist."

Moral of the story: Always remember and honor those who have gone before you.

MORE DAD'S COLLEGE ADVICE

One day, when they were still Jedi college students, Yoda and Obi Wan were travelling in a space ship.

Obi Wan asks, "Are we going the right way?"

Yoda answers, "Off course, we are."

Moral of the story: Whenever answering a question make sure you give a clear answer whose meaning cannot be interpreted with ambiguity.

MORE DAD'S COLLEGE ADVICE

A college student was picking up his girlfriend's mother from the airport.

He asked her, "So, how long do you think you'll be staying with us?"

She answered, "Well... for as long as you like."

"Not even for coffee??"

Moral of the story: Be a good and gracious host to your visitors; you may need them to return the favor one day.

MORE DAD'S COLLEGE ADVICE

A college student came back to his room looking very disheveled.

"What on earth happened to you?" asked his roommate.

In a trembling voice he replied, "I was attacked by a group of mimes. They did unspeakable things to me."

"Well, if you're ever attacked by them again, just remember to go for the juggler."

Moral of the story: Use the buddy system when walking across campus, especially at night.

MORE DAD'S COLLEGE ADVICE

A Scottish college student phones in sick to work.

His boss asks, "What's wrong Jimmy?"

Jimmy replies, "I have a wee cough."

Boss says, "You have a wee cough?"

Jimmy says, "Thank you, boss. I was only going to take one day."

Moral of the story: Taking care of your health is part of being responsible to your work.

MORE DAD'S COLLEGE ADVICE

As two college students were driving down the road, the song "Sweet Caroline" came on the radio.

The first student said, "Little known fact, Neil Diamond used to be called Neil Coal."

"Really?"

"Yep. Until the pressure got to him."

Moral of the story: Nothing is worth going into a panic; and if you remain composed and work well under pressure, then you can be the calm in the storm for others.

MORE DAD'S COLLEGE ADVICE

A stuffy college professor goes out and buys the best car on the market, a brand new Ferrari GTO. It is also an incredibly expensive car, and it costs him over $500,000. He takes it out for a spin to show it off, and stops at a red light. A college student on a moped, pulls up next to him.

The college student looks over at the sleek shiny car and asks, "What kind of car ya got there, prof?"

The college professor smugly replies, "A Ferrari GTO. It cost half a million dollars!"

"That's a lot of money," says the college student. "Why does it cost so much?"

"Because this car can do up to 250 miles an hour!" states the college professor proudly.

The moped driver asks, "Mind if I take a look inside?"

"No problem," replies the college professor.

So the college student pokes his head in the window and looks around. Then, sitting back on his moped, the college student says, "That's a pretty nice car, all right, but I'll stick with my moped!"

Just then the light changes, so the college professor decides to show the college student just what his car can do. He floors it, and almost instantaneously, the speedometer reads 150 mph.

Suddenly, he notices a dot in his rear view mirror – and wonders what it could be, when suddenly he hears a loud "WHHHOOOOOOSSSSSHHH!" And something whips by him going much faster!

"What on earth could be going faster than my Ferrari?" the college professor asks himself.

He floors the accelerator and takes the Ferrari up to 175 mph. Then, up ahead of him, he sees that it's the college student on the moped!

Amazed that the moped could pass his Ferrari, he gives it more gas and passes the moped at 210 mph.

He's feeling pretty good until he looks in his mirror and sees the college student gaining on him AGAIN!

Astounded by the speed of the college student, he floors the gas pedal and takes the Ferrari all the way up to 250 mph.

Not ten seconds later, he sees the moped bearing down on him again! The Ferrari is topped out, and there's nothing he can do to go faster!

Suddenly, the moped plows into the back of his Ferrari, demolishing the rear end.

The college professor stops and jumps out and, unbelievably, the college student is still alive. He runs up to the mangled college student and says, "Oh my gosh! Is there anything I can do for you?"

The college student whispers, "Unhook my suspenders from your side mirror."

Moral of the story: Always wear your seatbelt; suspenders are optional.

MORE DAD'S COLLEGE ADVICE

A graduate student went on a date with a blonde college student one night.

"Do you have any kids?" she asked.

"Yes," he replied. "I have one child that's just under two."

She replied indignantly, "I might be blonde, but I know how many one is."

Moral of the story: Don't assume someone is talking down to you just because they are explaining things to you.

MORE DAD'S COLLEGE ADVICE

The local Department of Transportation found over 200 dead crows on highways recently, and there was a concern that they may have died from Avian Flu.

A pathologist from the local university examined the remains of all the crows, and, to everyone's relief, confirmed the problem was NOT Avian Flu.

So they commissioned an analysis to be done by a group of local college graduate students. The cause of death appeared to be from vehicular impacts. However, during analysis it was noted that varying colors of paints appeared on the birds' beaks and claws.

By analyzing these paint residues it was found that 98% of the crows had been killed by impacts with motorcycles, while only 2% were killed by impacts with cars.

The group then brought in additional ornithological behaviorist students to determine if there was a reason for the disproportionate percentages of motorcycle kills versus car kills.

The ornithological behaviorists quickly found that when crows eat road kill, they always post a look-out crow to warn of danger. They also discovered that while all the lookout crows could shout "CAH, CAH", not a single one of them could shout "MOTORCYCLE".

Moral of the story: If you've got something important to say, don't be shy about making sure that people understand what you are saying.

MORE DAD'S COLLEGE ADVICE

A college student was telling her roommate about her day.

She said, "Today I saw a little boy wearing rags sitting on a curb. I said, 'Awww, are you an orphan?'"

He said, "Yes, what gave me away?"

I said, "Your parents."

Moral of the story: Be nice and patient with others; not everyone comes from the same situation.

MORE DAD'S COLLEGE ADVICE

Two college students were studying for their Spanish final by asking each other questions.

The first asked, "What do you call four Mexicans in quicksand?"

The other answered, "Quatro sinko."

Moral of the story: It's good to learn about other countries and the holidays they celebrate, like Cinco de Mayo.

MORE DAD'S COLLEGE ADVICE

Two college students were having lunch one day. Over the course of their meal the first began complaining about his neighbor.

"My neighbor was bashing on my door at 2 AM this morning! Just bashing and bashing on my door! Can you believe the nerve of doing something like that?!"

"Wow," his friend replied, "how extremely rude."

"I know, right!?! Lucky for him I was still up playing my drums."

Moral of the story: Be a good neighbor; good neighbors are worth their weight in gold.

MORE DAD'S COLLEGE ADVICE

Two college students were having lunch one day.

The first asked, "Hey, how did your big fancy weekend go?"

"Not so good, man."

"Why not so good? What went wrong?"

"You know how I wanted to celebrate my first big paycheck?"

"Yes. You did get paid didn't you?"

"Oh, yeah. And not only did I get paid my regular check, but I also got a huge bonus check. I was ready to go out partying and spend it all just having a good time out on the town."

"Then why didn't you?"

"Well, I made a mistake of paying $350 for a limo, but then found out that it didn't include a driver. So I was stuck at home by myself with a pile of cash . . . . . all that money and nothing to chauffeur it."

Moral of the story: Read the fine print before you sign on the dotted line.

MORE DAD'S COLLEGE ADVICE

A college student asked her roommate, "What do you know about bonsai trees?"

Her roommate sat quietly thinking for a moment before answering, "Very little."

Moral of the story: Don't overcomplicate things. Sometimes it's best to use the 'KISS' method . . . . keep it short and simple.

MORE DAD'S COLLEGE ADVICE

Two college students were discussing their past relationships.

The first one said, "I think my ex-girlfriend has weekly lessons with the devil on how to be more evil. I don't know what she charges him though."

Moral of the story: Don't badmouth people behind their back; it makes you look petty.

MORE DAD'S COLLEGE ADVICE

A bald eagle, who happened to be a college student, decides to stop by a small lake to get a drink.

As he's drinking, another bald eagle, who also happens to be a college student, lands next to him.

The first one looks at the second eagle and notices a tulip, a rose, and a rabbit's foot on top of his head.

"What's with the stuff on your head?" the first eagle asks.

"Oh this?" the second says while pointing to his head with his wing, "I'm trying hare in plants."

Moral of the story: Everyone is different; don't judge harshly lest you be judged harshly also.

MORE DAD'S COLLEGE ADVICE

Two college students were talking about their families one day. The first one talked about his grandfather.

"My grandad always said 'When one door closes, another opens.' He was an awesome guy, but he was a terrible cabinetmaker."

Moral of the story: Things will always work out okay, just not always according to your plans, but instead according to God's plans. So put your worries in His hands.

ABOUT THE AUTHOR

The author is a middle age Midwestern father of four who, at the end of one summer, suddenly found himself with three kids attending college. During that school year, he would send a nightly text message to his kids. This book is a collection of those messages. Each message contained two parts. The first part was always a bit of humor, to help the students deal with the stress of being away from home. The second part was a "Moral of the story" to help the dad feel like he was imparting "fatherly advice" without lecturing his kids. The jokes are not his own, although he did tweak them to fit this purpose. He hopes that this collection will help other children, and their fathers, reduce stress levels as they travel along through life.

www.ingramcontent.com/pod-product-compliance
Lightning Source LLC
LaVergne TN
LVHW041212080426
835508LV00011B/916